Managing

INFORMATION

TECHNOLOGY

Projects

MANAGING

INFORMATION

TECHNOLOGY

PROJECTS

**Applying Project Management Strategies to
Software, Hardware, and Integration Initiatives**

James Taylor

AMACOM

American Management Association
New York • Atlanta • Brussels • Chicago • Mexico City • San Francisco
Shanghai • Tokyo • Toronto • Washington, D.C.

Special discounts on bulk quantities of AMACOM books are available to corporations, professional associations, and other organizations. For details, contact Special Sales Department, AMACOM, a division of American Management Association, 1601 Broadway, New York, NY 10019.
Tel.: 212-903-8316. Fax: 212-903-8083.
Web site: www.amacombooks.org

This publication is designed to provide accurate and authoritative information in regard to the subject matter covered. It is sold with the understanding that the publisher is not engaged in rendering legal, accounting, or other professional service. If legal advice or other expert assistance is required, the services of a competent professional person should be sought.

"PMI" and the PMI logo are service and trademarks registered in the United States and other nations; "PMP" and the PMP logo are certification marks registered in the United States and other nations; "PMBOK," "PM Network," and "PMI Today" are trademarks registered in the United States and other nations; and "Project Management Journal" and "Building professionalism in project management" are trademarks of the Project Management Institute, Inc.

Library of Congress Cataloging-in-Publication Data

Taylor, James
       Managing information technology projects : applying project management strategies to software, hardware, and integration initiatives / James Taylor.
            p.   cm.
       Includes index.
       ISBN 0-8144-0811-7
       1. Project management.   2. Information technology—Management.   3. Management information systems.   I. Title.

HD69.P75T386 2004
004'.068'4—dc21

2003008645

Printing number

10   9   8   7   6   5   4   3   2   1

To Karen Romano-Taylor,

my wife and best friend.

Thank you for your love, support, and patience.

Contents

List of Exhibits

Acknowledgments

This book is the product of many years in public and private industry learning to manage projects and organizations. Much of what I have learned about project management is the result of trying to teach or mentor others. It was well said by someone, "Learning is best achieved through teaching." I have also grown intellectually, as well as professionally, through my seven-year association with ESI International—first as an instructor of their fine project management courses and now as a full-time employee responsible for ensuring that our courses teach the most current project management perspectives, techniques, and tools. I am especially grateful to my ESI colleagues who patiently listen to my theories and opinions and who are so artful at helping me crystallize my thoughts. And finally I wish to thank ESI senior management for their encouragement to write this book and for their help in providing me with information and resources to accompany my research into the many facets of project management.

Chapter 1

Introduction

Studies consistently show that 80–90 percent of all software and 30–45 percent of all systems projects fail. Moreover, over half of all systems projects overrun their budgets and schedules by up to 200 percent or more. Of the projects that fail, approximately half of all those that are restarted fail again. Yet management tools and techniques, as well as software development techniques, are constantly improving. What are the causes of these expensive and seemingly uncontrollable failures?

One explanation for these high failure rates lies in the definition of failure. To a developer or an engineer, a project may be successful if the deliverables are provided to the customer regardless of schedule or budget considerations. Senior management may consider the same project a failure if it does not turn a profit, even if it is completed on time and budget. But that is splitting hairs. Project success or failure is not a matter of semantics. A project is a success only if it delivers the product or service on time, on budget, to the customer's prescribed requirements, and if its financial returns, positive or negative, are consistent with the company's strategic plan. Generally, projects succeed or fail according to how robust and viable the project management process is at the performing organization.

1

The Project Management Process

Computerworld, a leading systems magazine, published the results of several surveys regarding project management process deficiencies. Their results show what was missing at the surveyed companies where project failure was a major problem. The most significant problems revealed a lack of:

- ✔ A project office or a clearly defined project organization (42 percent)
- ✔ Integrated methods (41 percent)
- ✔ Training and mentoring (38 percent)
- ✔ Policies and procedures (35 percent)
- ✔ Implementation plans (23 percent)
- ✔ Executive support (22 percent)

The elements of a project management process and basic project management tools are essentially the same whether the project is in the information technology (IT) environment, construction environment, or some other engineering project environment. And therein lies the problem; the processes and tools are essentially the same, but the projects are not. Too many organizations and project managers still attempt to manage IT projects as if they were engineering or construction projects. To successfully manage IT projects, the management approach must be updated to reflect the current business environment, and the management processes and tools must be adapted to account for the specific characteristics of the IT environment.

What Is IT?

There are several excellent books that provide basic project management information. These books or similar ones were sufficient until IT charged into the business world. Generic approaches to project management (i.e., general tutorials on basic project management tools such as the work breakdown structure, network analysis, Gantt charts, and earned value) serve the general project management community well. With the emergence of IT, though, the literature has not kept pace, and project managers are desperately trying to apply the generic tools to IT with little or no success. The few authors who have attempted to fill the project management knowledge gap made progress but fell short. Today, most IT project management books only address the software development component of the information technology equation. The result is a significant step forward, but it fails to address IT as a system. There are two major problems at the root of IT project failures:

The management approach must be changed from old or traditional project management thinking, and IT has to be addressed as a total system.

This book defines IT to include not only computer technology, both the software and hardware components, but also the integration of these subsystems into a total, functional, and usable system. The total IT system will contain two or more of the following: software, hardware, communications, training, conversion or migration, and deployment of the system.

Managing an IT project means managing the total effort and ensuring that the various components integrate to produce the desired final product. Focusing on either one of these components exclusively is bound to end in failure. It also brings forth these questions: How does the current management approach differ from the old? What are the implications relative to organizational support?

Project Management: Then and Now

The art and science of project management has changed radically over the last twenty years. Projects of yesteryear, even large and complex ones, had some characteristics that made them easier to manage. They usually were stand-alone projects having dedicated

resources, and many of them did not have the disastrous consequences of not meeting a rush-to-market window. For example,
as late as 1970, the average length of time from operational concept to fielding a military airplane was between fifteen and twenty
years. After being placed in service, these aircraft are operationally
effective for between twenty and fifty years.

Many engineering and construction projects still are best managed in the traditional fashion. However, with the beginning of
software development and the increasing numbers of other high-
tech projects, the old tools and techniques were found to be less
efficient, even counterproductive, if used in the traditional way. To
exacerbate this problem, in the mid-to-late 1980s and early 1990s,
companies began to reengineer themselves to become more efficient with fewer resources, which was in response to an increasingly
competitive marketplace. Consequently, the concept of dedicated
project resources was no longer viable, requiring a different look at
the organizational structure and operation. New approaches and
techniques in managing complex, fast-paced, and ever-changing
projects were needed, which brings us to the present.

The need for new and better techniques has grown faster
than they can be developed or implemented. Nevertheless, companies are still attempting to manage high-tech projects using old
tools and concepts. An understanding of the differences in the
traditional approach to project management and what is now
needed is crucial before a viable and successful IT project management process can be implemented. Understanding how IT projects differ from other project types helps define a process for
successfully managing them.

The IT Project: How Is It Different?

Intuitively, organizations and project teams have always felt that
IT projects are different and therefore must have a unique set of
project management tools and techniques to accomplish them.
However, project management techniques and tools can apply to
any project in any industry, regardless of whether it involves software, hardware, construction, engineering, or services. It is not

the tools that are different, but rather the projects. What make IT projects different are their unique risks, the rapid development requirements to meet rush-to-market demands, the short life of technology, and multiple dependencies with other projects. So the tools are the same, but they must be applied differently depending upon the project type and complexity.

It is true that several techniques have been developed that shorten software development cycles, but these techniques are process-oriented, so they are not classified as tools—they apply equally well to other industries. Even so, it is important to understand these techniques and how to apply them in IT projects. Several of the most common rapid development tools are discussed in Chapter 10.

A comparison of general characteristics of IT and non–IT or traditional projects is shown in Exhibit 1-1. These characteristics are discussed throughout the book, but graphically showing how IT projects differ will help to focus your thinking on how to apply the project management tools and techniques as they are discussed in the following chapters. Discovery of how these tools and techniques are applied will benefit several different individuals, functional organizations, and the organization as a whole.

Who This Book Will Benefit

This book is primarily written for project managers who are responsible for IT projects. However, because the management tools and techniques are applicable to any project, anyone responsible for projects, particularly projects with multiple interfaces and system integration requirements, will benefit from this study.

The book is written primarily for the beginning project manager, but at a level and organization so that more experienced project managers will find new ideas and tips for better managing their projects. It will also serve as a good review for all project managers who have an interest in sharpening their skills or who are preparing to take the Project Management Institute (PMI) certification examination.

Project Component	Non–IT Project	IT Project
Project	Not integrated with most business functions	Usually linked with business processes and organizations systems
Project structure	Often stand alone	Usually multiple projects with numerous interdependencies
Scope	Well defined	Less defined and subject to change
Change control	Well defined	Definable change control process but more difficult to track
Stakeholders	Fewer; easier to identify	More; more difficult to identify
Staffing/resources	Often full-time (depends upon organizational structure)	Usually part-time; skill sets used as task progress dictates
Staffing	Best people in critical skill sets; average in others; more generalists	Best people available; mostly specialists
Large projects	Divide by organization or establish stand-alone unit	Allocated by specialty (risk areas) across organizational lines
Risk	More easily identified; poorly managed but usually with less negative impact	Not easily identified; poorly managed with high project/organizational impact
Metrics documentation	Poor to fair	Moderately good, but poorly applied
Lessons learned	Poor to fair	Poor
Budget and schedule estimation	Good	Poor

Exhibit 1-1. A comparison of IT and non–IT project characteristics.

This book will also benefit functional and other senior managers who are striving to develop a project-oriented organization. There are numerous tips and suggestions throughout the book for structuring support processes and the guidelines required for successful project management.

How This Book Is Organized

The chapters in this book closely follow the phases of a typical project and system development life cycle. In addition, the chapters can be grouped into logical sections. The first section, Chapters 1 through 3, discusses the project management basics, the project and systems development life cycle and how they relate, and the project management and team activities of both cycles. The second section, Chapters 4 through 6, discusses how to analyze and plan the project. The third section, Chapter 7, discusses risk management in the IT environment. The fourth section, Chapter 8, introduces the reader to basic project integration concepts by explaining systems engineering concepts. The fifth section, Chapters 9 and 10, discusses project control and rapid development techniques. Finally, the sixth section, Chapters 11 and 12, deals with what are often the most difficult phases of a project, project: close out and customer service after project completion.

Learning Objectives of This Book

Project management has become a career path for many industries. Not too many years ago, the way one could progress in the corporate structure was either through the finance or new business development ladder. Since the late 1980s, though, organizations have become more project-oriented in their approach to business, and project management training and certification have taken on a new meaning and importance. Many private and public sector organizations now require that their employees be certified before they can fill the role of project manager. The Project Management

Institute is the certifying organization for the Project Management Professional (PMP).

The primary objective of this book is to provide the reader with a fundamental understanding of project management in the IT environment and the tools to successfully complete an IT project. Although project management tools and techniques are applicable to any type of project, each project has a unique requirement that can change how the tools are used. This book will discuss these different applications.

The second most important objective is to explain that the software development life cycle (SDLC) is a subset of the project life cycle and to show how they fit together. As a part of the discussion on SDLC, this book discusses the specialized tools of software development and how they fit into the project management techniques and tools.

A third objective is to demonstrate that IT is not just software development. It is important to IT project management success that we understand the components of the IT environment, how they all fit and operate together, and how to plan, implement, control, and deliver the IT product. This book will demonstrate how this is done.

The Project Management Institute

This book is written to be consistent with the standards and principles of the Project Management Institute and the Project Management Body of Knowledge (PMBOK) as much as possible. However, my desire is to present best practice perspectives, techniques, and tools, which may differ from PMI's approach. It should be remembered that PMI's standards are based on how *most* professional project managers view project management. At the same time, PMI recognizes that project management is not entirely prescriptive and that there are other solutions to management problems. I have endeavored to note any such differences of opinion, but it should be remembered that, for purposes of preparing for the PMP examination, PMI's viewpoint prevails.

Chapter 2

The Foundations of Project Management

Project management, in some form, has existed for thousands of years. Some notable examples are the great pyramids, Moses' movement of the Israelites out of Egypt, the temple and palace built by Solomon, and the magnificent building programs of the Greeks and the Romans. How these projects were accomplished at all defies imagination, particularly given the tools of the day. For instance, how was the Great Pyramid of Cheops, consisting of an estimated 2,300,000 stone blocks, weighing two to seventy tons each, built with such precision? This pyramid, the size of a forty-story building, stands on a thirteen-acre base that even today deviates less than an inch off level.

With the advent of electricity and industrialization, project complexity increased. No longer were projects complex principally because they were large-scale exercises in endurance. Now they were complex because of their scale. In addition, because of component complexity, they demanded improved project management techniques and tools. The catalyst for these improvements was World War II and the resulting cold war.

World War II brought a refinement to project management that had never been experienced. Manufacturing and production lines were optimized for producing war materials faster and better.

Management of these efforts required new and better project management techniques, resulting in a surge of new thinking in project management. The United States Department of Defense (DOD) began to develop or contract for new and better tools and techniques for managing projects. Projects such as the Polaris submarine involved so many contractors and so much development that it was virtually impossible to schedule or track progress using standard management techniques. Thus, scheduling and network analysis techniques were developed to provide consistent project tracking and controlling techniques. Consequently, the DOD is directly responsible for introducing nearly all the traditional project management tools used by professional project managers today.

IT projects have created more project management challenges. To exacerbate the challenge of project complexity, nearly all IT projects have the added constraint of tighter schedules, usually imposed by the need to rush to market.

IT is pervasive. The technological fuel for this pervasiveness is not just the computer. It is the marriage of computer technology with communication technology. The explosion of IT onto the world has solved many business problems and opened new business directions, but it has also created some serious management issues.

IT Benefits and Issues

One of the major benefits of IT is that companies now have the ability to communicate rapidly across organizational, national, and international lines, making it the backbone of virtually every business today. With this newfound capability, every company has the opportunity to make their management processes more effective and efficient. Unfortunately, many businesses do not have the expertise or cultural inclination to make the changes required. It is a major challenge to adapt management and support processes to keep pace with IT changes.

The track record for managing IT projects is not good, and the principal reason is the lack of project planning brought on by the need to rush to market, which creates the perception of limited or no planning time. Another reason is the lack of organizational commitment to becoming a project-oriented organization, which requires, among other things, a formal and documented management process, a specially selected and trained project management cadre, and the understanding and use of standard project management tools. Project management processes and project manager selection and characteristics are discussed in the next chapter.

Fundamental Definitions in a Project-Oriented Environment

To ensure a common understanding of project management tools, this chapter will define some basic project-oriented terms and will discuss four of project management's most important tools: the work breakdown structure (WBS), the Gantt chart, network diagramming, and earned value. These important tools are the foundations of project management regardless of the type project.

Project and Project Management

A project is usually a onetime activity with a well-defined set of desired end results. It is this onetime characteristic that differentiates project activities from functional activities. For example, individuals in a functional department, such as human resources, may have specific projects assigned to them, but their usual responsibilities are recurring. A project is defined as a unique, temporary effort to produce specific deliverables measured against customer-specified performance criteria.

Project Uniqueness

Every project is unique. No two projects are alike, regardless of how routine they are to the organization. Each one is characterized by some degree of customization. Even if two projects were exactly alike technically, differences would be noticeable because the four parties at interest, or stakeholders (i.e., client or customer, parent organization, project team, and the public), define success or failure in different ways. In addition, the stakeholder group is usually different for each project.

Temporary Duration

In the context of project duration, the term "temporary" is dependent on the industry or one's perception of time. For example, in the construction industry, a house might be built in six months, while a hospital might take two years to build. In the aerospace industry, a new aircraft development effort can take ten or more years. So temporary doesn't mean short-term as we generally use it, but rather it means that there are definite beginning and end points to the effort.

Customer-Specified Performance Criteria

The customer, whether internal or external, defines the level of performance required for the project deliverables. The customer or client defines these performance criteria in terms of requirements. It is the responsibility of the project manager to interpret the requirements and to obtain agreement from the customer that the interpretation accurately reflects the customer's needs. It is also the responsibility of the project manager to identify or develop standards against which to measure whether these requirements are met.

In some instances, industry standards can be used to measure performance criteria. For example, electrical codes exist for those projects requiring electrical wiring or power connections. Sometimes standards are a part of the performance criteria. For instance, a requirement of mean-time-between-failure (MTBF) of some number of hours can also serve as a standard. This is because MTBF is a quantifiable measure and can be identified with average acceptable values for similar systems. When standards are not available, the project manager is responsible for providing a way to determine whether the product is acceptable to the customer. One way might be to use an independent quality assurance group. Another way might be to write a standard or to use another company's product as a benchmark. The key to success in identifying, interpreting, and measuring customer requirements is to obtain customer input and agreement about your interpretation of these requirements and about how your performance will be measured.

Project Management Defined

Project management is a specialized approach to managing business. The traditional view of management is that we plan, organize, lead, and control the business process. Project management includes these functions but also includes project initiation and termination. Both traditional and project management processes are shown graphically in Exhibits 2-1 and 2-2, respectively. We can define project management as the art and science of managing projects to a specific schedule, at or below a predetermined budget, to the customer's performance requirements and within the resources available.

Project management is both an art and a science. It is an art because it involves strong interrelationships with diverse groups. This part of project management is actually what makes it so challenging. Generally, the bigger project problems are those associated with the human element: conflict resolution, team building, and negotiating. Technical problems are far easier to solve than human problems. These technical tools make project management partly a science.

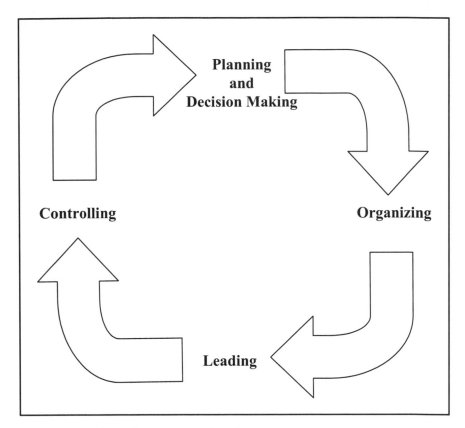

Exhibit 2-1. Traditional management functions.

There are many project management tools. Some are simple one-page forms. Others involve relatively complex calculations. Many of these tools are presented in this book, but the four most important ones are the WBS, the Gantt chart, network analysis, and earned value.

The Work Breakdown Structure

WBS is the most important project management tool. With a good WBS, the project manager can develop every other tool needed to successfully manage the project. When done correctly, it is the basis for planning, scheduling, budgeting, and controlling the project.

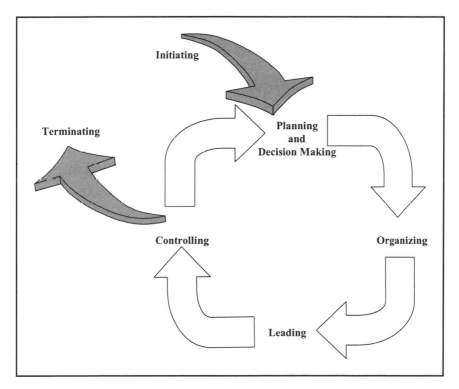

Exhibit 2-2. Project management functions.

What Is a Work Breakdown Structure?

A WBS is a structured way of decomposing a project into its various components—software, hardware, communications network, services, documentation, labor, testing, implementation, installation, and maintenance. In short, WBS is a formalized way of reducing the project into successively lower levels of greater detail.

There are two ways to represent a WBS. The first and most popular form is called the indented format. The indented format derives its name from the practice of indenting each successively lower level, as shown in Exhibit 2-3.

The graphical format, shown in Exhibit 2-4, resembles an organizational chart and is especially helpful for those who prefer visual representations. However, it requires a lot of space to de-

WBS Number	Description	WBS Level
1.0	Project or Contract Name	1
1.1	Major Project Subdivision	2
1.1.1	Task	3
1.1.1.1	Subtask	4
1.1.1.1.1	Work Package	5
1.1.1.1.1.1	Components	6

Exhibit 2-3. Indented WBS.

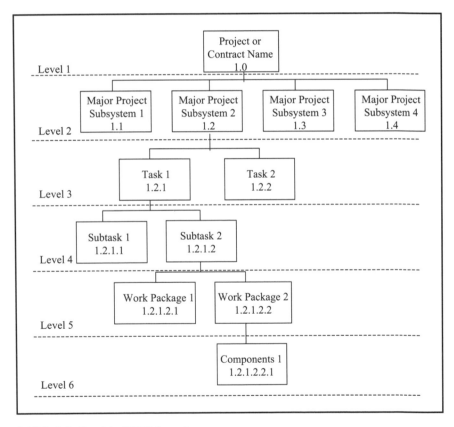

Exhibit 2-4. Graphical WBS format.

velop, particularly for large, complex projects. Not all project management software supports the graphical format, but all of them support the indented representation.

The WBS Levels

WBS levels refer to the successively lower tiers of detail beginning with the project name as the first level. Usually, a WBS is developed to the third or fourth level but rarely needs to be developed below the fifth level. There are two key points in WBS development. First, the level of development has nothing to do with the type of project, the industry, or the customer—private or public. It has to do with the complexity of the project. A WBS to the third level can easily describe a simple project of a few tasks. But a project such as building a house, hospital, or airplane requires a detailed WBS to at least the fifth level.

The WBS Levels Described

Each of the WBS levels are described as follows:

- ✔ *Level One.* The project or contract name is always at this level.
- ✔ *Level Two.* Entries involving the major subsystems of the project, complete entities, or sections of the project are at this level. For example, the major subsystems of an automobile design project would include the engine, chassis, interior, and body.
- ✔ *Level Three.* Each level two entry also can consist of one or more major task activities. For example, if the level two subsystem is the engine, tasks might be the fan or carburetor, which are parts of the engine. These are designated as level three activities.
- ✔ *Level Four.* Each level three activity can be decomposed into several more discrete entities, and so on, until the desired level

of detail is achieved. For example, a subtask of the carburetor would be to design and build fuel jets. These level three subtasks are all entered into the WBS at level four.

✔ **Level Five.** Decomposing level four tasks usually brings us to a level where the actual work can be assigned: the work package. The work package is identifiable with a person, a job, or a budget number and is where the actual project work is accomplished. The work package can occur anywhere below the first level, but usually occurs at the fourth or fifth level. The idea is to define the work package at a level where the project manager is comfortable that he can manage the work.

An example of a fifth-level work package is the subtask of defining a valve for the fuel jets described at level four. This is a discrete work package, which can be given to an individual or group. Now a schedule and budget for the effort can be assigned.

A sample WBS is presented in Exhibit 2-5. Several key points about this example should be noted. First, the name of the project is at the first level. Second, not every major subsystem or subproject is decomposed to the same level. It is only necessary to decompose the elements of the WBS to the level at which it is possible to assign individuals, a budget, and a schedule to the task. Each project manager will have a different view of the required level of WBS decomposition. My level of comfort, relative to managing the project, might require that I decompose all the WBS elements to the fourth level, while you may be comfortable operating at the third level. The third thing to note about the sample WBS is that the lowest levels—that is, work packages—are described by a verb, while nouns describe higher levels. This rule of thumb is helpful in developing a WBS—when the element can be introduced by a verb; for example, develop, build, write, document. Then it probably is a work package and need not be decomposed to a lower level.

Note in Exhibit 2-5 that I included the project management

1.0 Management Information Software System
    1.1. Gap Analysis
        1.1.1. Needs assessment
            1.1.1.1. Measure state of current system.
            1.1.1.2. Determine additional capability requirements.
        1.1.2. Develop alternative approaches.
    1.2. Requirements Specifications
        1.2.1. Develop preliminary software specifications.
        1.2.2. Develop detailed software specifications.
        1.2.3. Develop preliminary hardware specifications.
    1.3. Systems Engineering
        1.3.1. Develop alternative software approaches.
        1.3.2. Develop alternative hardware approaches.
        1.3.3. Develop cost estimates for each alternative approach.
        1.3.4. Determine best technical and most cost-effective approach.
        1.3.5. Develop preferred system architecture.
    1.4. System Design
        1.4.1. Develop preliminary system design.
            1.4.1.1. Design software modules.
            1.4.1.2. Design hardware subsystems.
            1.4.1.3. Integrate systems.
            1.4.1.4. Develop detailed system design.
    1.5. System Development
        1.5.1. Write code for system modules.
        1.5.2. Construct hardware subsystems.
        1.5.3. Develop prototype.
    1.6. Testing
        1.6.1. Write test plans.
        1.6.2. Test units.
            1.6.2.1. Test code.
            1.6.2.2. Modify code.
            1.6.2.3. Test hardware.
            1.6.2.4. Modify hardware.
        1.6.3. System testing.
            1.6.3.1. Integrate system.
            1.6.3.2. Test code.
            1.6.3.3. Modify code.
            1.6.3.4. Test hardware.
            1.6.3.5. Modify hardware.
        1.6.4. Prototype tests.
            1.6.4.1. Conduct prototype tests.
            1.6.4.2. Document test results.
            1.6.4.3. Modify module code/hardware.
    1.7. Develop Production Model
        1.7.1. Develop production tests.
            1.7.1.1. Conduct tests.
            1.7.1.2. Document test results.
        1.7.2. Conduct deployment.
            1.7.2.1. Deliver system.
            1.7.2.2. Install system.
        1.7.3. Maintain system.
            1.7.3.1. Detect/correct faults.
            1.7.3.2. Modify/enhance system.
    1.8. Project Management
        1.8.1. Assign project manager.
        1.8.2. Assign project engineer.
        1.8.3. Assign administrative assistant.
        1.8.4. Assign cost analyst.

Exhibit 2-5. Sample work breakdown structure.

functions as a line item entry. Although these functions are not tasks in the context of usual WBS elements, listing them is a good way to collect costs associated with the project management activity. Otherwise, the cost of project management time must be spread across each task in the project, a formidable effort. Therefore, rather than apportioning the project manager's time to every single task, it is much easier to include a separate WBS entry and provide one total cost for the estimated project duration.

The primary objective in developing a WBS is to ensure that every project task is identified. It is not an objective to determine or record the interdependencies of the tasks at this point. In fact, it is better not to think in terms of task dependencies until all tasks are identified. Concentrate on identifying all the tasks first, because if it is not in the WBS, it is not in the project. The network is the tool used to show task relationships.

Network Analysis

Networks have been used since the early 1950s, when Lockheed and Booz Allen Hamilton developed the project evaluation review technique (PERT) for the Navy's Polaris missile program. Since then, several other network techniques have been developed to compensate for some shortcomings in the PERT method and to provide additional capabilities. Although the PERT network method is still used occasionally, the most common network analysis technique is the precedence diagram method (PDM). This technique eliminates some of the problems with PERT, but it owes its popularity to Microsoft Project and other project management software because it is easier to program. Since PDM is the generally preferred and used network tool, only its development and analysis is shown in this chapter. However, the PERT technique will be discussed in Chapter 6 as a risk mitigation tool. You can find more detailed discussions of PERT and other networking techniques in most basic project management texts.

The first step in developing the project schedule is to estimate the duration of each individual task. Duration estimation should include any contingencies to plan against potential resource shortages. That is, the best-case scenario should not be assumed for the duration—neither should the worst-case scenario. The duration is usually taken to be the average of similar tasks from the organization's historical database. But those tasks at risk, relative to potentially unavailable resource numbers or skills, should be planned with a contingency factor. One of the major benefits of the PDM method is that it can accommodate and track this kind of planning, whereas the PERT method cannot.

Task leaders typically estimate duration and labor requirements, but some organizations prefer that the functional managers make those estimates, since they are the ones who allocate resources and better understand project priorities. Once all task durations are estimated, the next step is to determine task interdependencies.

Determining task interdependencies is a team effort because each task leader will better understand what she needs as output from other tasks before she can finish her own effort. Task interdependencies drive the schedule because some tasks simply cannot begin until other tasks are completed. For example, the task of system design must be completed before system construction begins. On the other hand, some tasks have no dependencies and can be accomplished in parallel with other tasks. The testing of a completed subsystem, for example, can be accomplished while another subsystem is in development. So careful examination of task interdependencies can shorten the schedule, if two or more tasks are done at the same time rather than sequentially. However, doing this may add substantial risk to the project, which is the trade-off against potential schedule improvement.

For example, you may have planned a technology survey before designing a critical subsystem, but you may then decide to begin the design and survey at the same time in order to use the survey results to validate your understanding of the state of the available technology. If your knowledge of the available technology is current, this approach is viable and could improve the schedule significantly. However, if the survey comes back indicating that your choice of system components is obsolete, then not only have you not improved the schedule, but very likely you have created a schedule slip. Considering each task in turn, and its relationship to every other project task, results in a precedence table, as shown in Exhibit 2-6.

The precedence table lists the tasks of a project or a phase, the tasks that must be accomplished before each other task can begin, and the estimated duration of each. The precedence diagram is developed from the precedence table. Exhibit 2-7 is the PDM representation of the Exhibit 2-6 table information.

The alphabetical task identifiers are used purely for convenience so that the entire task description does not have to be written on the node. The task leader, taking into account the experiences of previous similar task efforts, usually determines the duration of each of the tasks. It is worth repeating that the task duration estimate takes resource availability into account. Otherwise the network analysis to determine the project schedule will be meaningless.

The first step in analyzing any network is to determine the

Task Alphabetical Identifier	WBS Tasks	Precedence	Task Duration (Weeks)
a	Develop system architecture.	—	4
b	Design software modules.	a	8
c	Write code.	b	12
d	Design hardware subsystems.	a	6
e	Build hardware subsystems.	d	4
f	Write test plans.	a	2
g	Test software.	c, f	2
h	Test hardware.	e, f	1
i	Integrate software and hardware.	g, h	3
j	Test system.	i	2
k	Install system.	j	1

Exhibit 2-6. Sample precedence table.

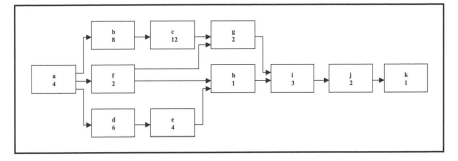

Exhibit 2-7. A precedence diagram.

early schedule—that is, the earliest each task can begin and end. The early schedule is determined by beginning at node a and working from left to right through each path. A path follows the arrows from the beginning to the end of the project. For example, tasks a, b, c, g, i, j, and k is a path. The early start (ES) and early finish (EF) of each task is recorded in the upper left and right corners, as shown in Exhibit 2-8. Starting at node a, the earliest the task can begin is at zero. The earliest it can finish is week four, since the estimated duration of the task is four weeks. The earliest that tasks b, f, and d can begin is after task a ends, or after the fourth week. Hence the early start for these three tasks is week four. Note that these times are accumulated times. That is, task b begins after a total of four weeks has been expended in the schedule. The early start for each task is the early finish of the preceding task, except when two or more tasks feed into it, such as at tasks g, h, and i. When two or more tasks feed into a succeeding task, then the early start time is the *larger* of the preceding early finish time possibilities. Hence, ES for task g is twenty-four weeks because the EF of task c is *larger* than the EF of task f. Finally, the EF of task k, thirty-two weeks, determines the schedule for the project. That is, thirty-two weeks is the earliest that the project can be accomplished given the available resources.

Determining the late schedule—that is, the latest a task can begin and end and still meet the estimated schedule of thirty-two weeks in the example—is done by working backward through the network. The late start (LS) and late finish (LF) times are re-

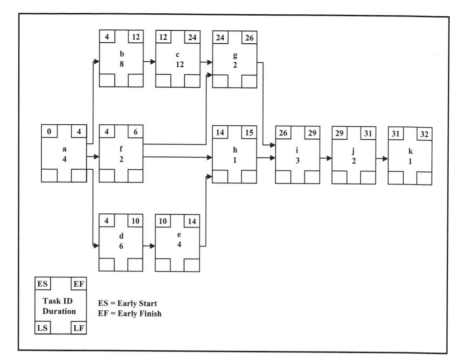

Exhibit 2-8. Network showing early schedule.

corded in the lower left and right corners of each node. To calculate LS and LF, begin at node k by recording thirty-two weeks in the LF box. The late finish of the last node is *always* the EF for that task because we want to determine how late the tasks can be started and ended *without* changing the estimated project schedule. The task duration is subtracted from the LF to obtain the LS for the task. Therefore, the late start for task k is thirty-one. The LF number for each task is the LS of the succeeding one. Thus, the LF for task j is thirty-one. The LS and LF for each task is calculated in the same manner backward through the network, except where two or more arrows back into a node. In those instances, such as for nodes f and a, then the LF is the *smaller* of the two LS possibilities. The completed network with the early and late schedules is shown in Exhibit 2-9. The heavy arrows indicate the critical path (i.e., the longest path through the network).

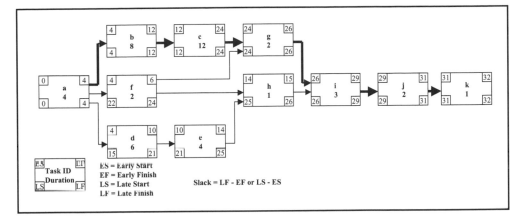

Exhibit 2-9. Completed network showing late schedule and critical path.

Slack (sometimes referred to as float) is calculated by subtracting the EF from the LF of a task. For example, the slack in task h is: LF – EF, which equals 26 – 15, which equals 11 weeks. Note that tasks a, b, c, g, i, j, and k do not have any slack. Not having slack on a path is also a defining characteristic of a critical path, and the tasks on it are called critical tasks. Critical in the context of network analysis means that if any one of those tasks slips, then the project schedule is affected. Hence, it is vital that these tasks be accomplished on time or ahead of schedule, but not later than planned.

The Gantt Chart

The WBS is the basis of all project schedules because it decomposes the project into the required tasks and allows the team to estimate each task's duration. The PDM provides a network showing the earliest and latest start and end times for each task and for the entire project. With that information at hand, Gantt charts can be prepared, graphically showing task, phase, and project schedules.

Henry L. Gantt, a pioneer in scientific management, developed the Gantt chart around 1917. It is a bar chart that shows planned and actual progress for a number of tasks displayed against a horizontal time scale. This type of information display is still one of the most effective and useful tools of project management. In addition to its use as a tracking tool for actual against planned progress, it is a very effective communications tool because it can portray a lot of data quickly to the interested parties. Exhibit 2-10 shows a sample of a Gantt chart using the WBS information from Exhibit 2-6. Although it was constructed with Microsoft Project, all other project packages produce similar schedules.

Projects are tracked and controlled using the Gantt schedules, earned value analysis, and change control processes. The change control process is discussed in Chapter 3 in detail, but earned value, the fourth major project tool, is discussed in the next section.

Earned Value

The basis of project control is still the WBS because it defines the project scope and describes the effort necessary to accomplish the project objectives. Earned value, which is a technique for tracking progress against actual accomplishment, is based on the WBS budget and schedule estimates. The Gantt chart facilitates the earned value analysis by providing a quick reference for percentage completion, a necessary input to the earned value formulas.

An earned value analysis is not particularly difficult from a mathematical viewpoint. The formulas are simple and require only straightforward arithmetic manipulations to arrive at a snapshot of how well the project is progressing. The difficulty is that it uses terms that are not familiar to us, and schedule is measured in terms of dollars instead of time. Since measuring schedule in this fashion goes against intuition and experience, some people focus on the language rather than the concepts of earned value, making learning to use the technique harder than it should be.

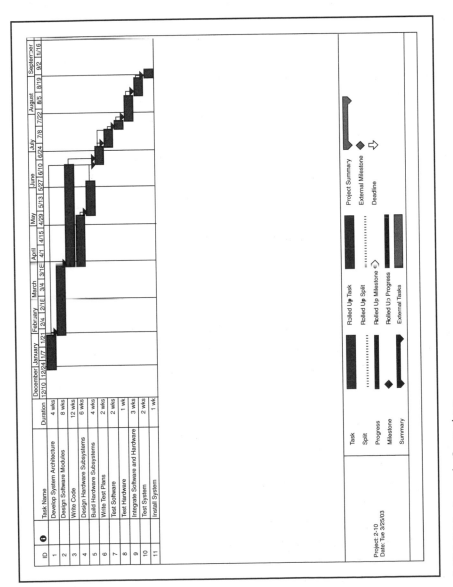

Exhibit 2-10. A sample Gantt chart.

The key to understanding earned value is in understanding three terms: planned value (PV), actual cost (AC), and work performed (EV). These three terms previously were known, respectively, as budgeted cost of work scheduled (BCWS), actual cost of work performed (ACWP), and budgeted cost of work performed (BCWP). EV is also known as the earned value, hence the origin of the name of this technique.

Once these three terms and the concepts behind them are mastered, the rest of earned value analysis is easy to understand and use.

Planned Value

PV is simply the task or project budget. Each task of the project has an estimated cost, so its PV is the amount of money identified for the expected or scheduled work to be done during execution. Each task has its own planned value. The accumulation of all these individual PV amounts equals the total budgeted cost for the project. Again, PV is an estimated amount and represents the cost that one expects to pay for part of a task, the whole task, or the project, depending on when in time the analysis is accomplished.

Actual Cost

AC is simply the amount of money that is actually paid out in the accomplishment of a task or the project. This figure is derived from labor, material, vendor, and subcontractor costs of the tasks as work on them progresses. Usually, the project manager is provided these figures from an accounting process that tracks invoices, accounts payable from vendors or subcontractors, and the salaries of personnel assigned to the tasks.

Before the earned value technique was developed in the late 1960s, AC and PV were the figures used to track project progress.

In other words, the project manager would compare actual and budgeted costs. If the actual costs were higher than expected expenditures, then it was assumed the project was in trouble. However, comparing actual and planned budget figures alone does not take schedule into account, so the project might actually be better off than expected. For example, if a project plan included the purchase of a number of computers during month five of the schedule, but the vendor offered them at a cheaper price to take them out of inventory earlier, then the actual costs for that period would be significantly higher than originally planned. Comparing only those figures would show the project to be over budget, but all else being equal, at month five the AC would be below the planned budget. In other words, more was spent at a point in time, but the project was way ahead of schedule. This concept introduces EV, the next and most difficult term to understand.

Earned Value

EV is the value of the work actually completed and measured against the planned completion amount for that period. Consider, for example, that a project is estimated to cost $20,000 and, for ease of calculation, that the cost across the project duration is linear. That is, at 25 percent completion, the project should cost $5,000; at 50 percent completion, $10,000; and so on. If the task progresses according to the planned schedule, then at the 25 percent progress point, the PV and the actual work accomplished is $5,000. That is, the budget for 25 percent of the work was planned to be $5,000 (PV), and since the task was on schedule at that point, then the budget for a completed 25 percent of work was also $5,000 (EV). But suppose at the time that this project was planned to be 25 percent completed, it was only 20 percent completed, or only 20 percent of the budgeted amount had been earned. Then the PV is $5,000 (25 percent of $20,000), and the EV is $4,000 (20 percent of $20,000). Hence, EV is a measure of schedule because it shows project progress—how much was accomplished against the plan.

Measurement or calculation of these three terms provides a basis for determining whether there is a cost and schedule variance from the project baseline.

Cost and Schedule Variance

Cost variance (CV) is the difference between the earned value and the actual cost of work performed. Mathematically, this relationship is expressed as:

$$CV = EV - AC$$

Schedule variance (SV) is the difference between the earned value and the planned value. The equation for SV is:

$$SV = EV - PV$$

Note that in both these equations, the first term on the right side of the equation is EV. EV is the key component for both these equations because this is the earned value term, or the amount earned toward completion of the project.

An example will better demonstrate the use of these formulas. Suppose at the planned 60 percent point for the $20,000 project, we actually have only completed 50 percent of the work. At this point, then, the PV is $12,000 and EV is $10,000. Suppose further that the actual moneys expended for the work accomplished is $8,000. The cost variance is:

$$CV = EV - AC$$
or
$$CV = 10,000 - 8,000$$
and
$$CV = \$2,000$$

A positive CV indicates that the project is under budget. A negative CV then indicates that the project is over budget. Of course, if the CV equals zero, then we are on budget.

The SV for this task is:

$$SV = EV - PV$$

or

$$SV = 10,000 - 12,000$$

and

$$SV = -\$2,000$$

A negative SV indicates that the project is behind schedule, a positive SV indicates that we are ahead of schedule, and a SV equal to zero means that we are exactly on schedule.

There are several other mathematical terms and equations important to the earned value techniques. These are the cost performance index (CPI), the schedule performance index (SPI), the budget at completion (BAC), the estimate to complete (ETC), and the estimate at completion (EAC). Each of these terms and their representative equations are discussed in detail below.

Schedule and Cost Performance Indexes

The SPI and CPI provide the same information as the SV and CV measures, except they are shown in terms of efficiency as opposed to pure numbers. This way of presenting the project status has some distinct advantages.

SPI is calculated by dividing the earned value by the planned value. Notice that these are the same components used to calculate schedule variance. Mathematically, SPI is represented by:

$$SPI = EV/PV$$

Or, using the previous example:

$$SPI = 10,000/12,000$$
$$SPI = 0.83 \text{ (rounded to the nearest 100th)}$$

If the SPI is less than 1.0, then it is behind schedule. If it is greater than 1.0, then it is ahead of schedule, and if it is 1.0, then it is exactly on track. Another way of looking at SPI is that for every dollar of physical work that the project planned to accomplish, only eighty-three cents was actually completed.

CPI is a measure of how much of the task or project value is earned against its actual cost to that point. It is calculated by dividing the earned value by the actual cost. Again, these are the same components used in the previous example to calculate the cost variance. Mathematically, CPI is described by:

$$CPI = EV/AC$$

or

$$CPI = 10,000/8,000$$

$$CPI = 1.25$$

The interpretation of CPI is that for every project dollar spent, \$1.25 of physical work is accomplished. That is, the project is earning more than it is spending.

Clearly, if CPI is less than 1.0, then the project is over budget (i.e., spending more to accomplish less). Likewise, if CPI is greater than 1.0, then the project is under budget, and a CPI equal to 1.0 shows the project is exactly on budget.

Both these indexes are more useful than the variance calculations for communicating progress to the stakeholders. A pure number (e.g., CV = − \$100) has no meaning to someone not intimately acquainted with the project and its finances because \$100 more or less gives no indication of how good or bad the project is doing. For example, if the EV is \$2,000 and the AC is \$2,100, the CV is still − \$100. But the CPI is now 0.95 (2,000/2,100), which indicates that the project is under budget, but not by very much relative to total amount earned or spent—and certainly not so much as to require drastic recovery actions. That is not true in a case where CV equals − \$100 and the CPI = 0.67, which occurs when EV is \$200 and AC is \$300. In the latter case, the project can only survive if drastic measures are not taken, and even then, the project will most likely not ever recover to a point of finishing on budget. Thus, the SPI and CPI indicators are excellent for use in status reporting and managing projects because they more accurately portray the true project status. These indexes also are important in predicting how much additional time or money may be needed to complete a project.

Estimates at Completion

The SPI and CPI are used to calculate final schedule and budget figures. For instance, suppose in our example the task originally was estimated to require ten weeks to complete. A new or latest schedule estimate (LSE) at completion can be calculated by dividing the original schedule at completion (SAC) estimate by the SPI. The latest schedule estimate is represented by:

$$LSE = SAC/SPI$$
or $$LSE = 10/0.83$$
$$LSE = 12.05 \text{ (rounded to nearest 100th)}$$

Hence, the new schedule requirement is just over twelve weeks if nothing is done to improve the schedule from this point forward.

Likewise, a latest revised budget estimate (LRE) is calculated by dividing the original budget at completion (BAC) by the CPI. Mathematically this calculation is provided by the equation:

$$LRE = BAC/CPI$$
or $$LRE = 20,000/1.25$$
$$LRE = \$16,000$$

So the new estimated cost of the total task is now $4,000 less than originally estimated. However, the CPI and SPI must be interpreted together. That is, the indication is that the project is under budget but behind schedule. This might be because some of the scheduled tasks are not completed or, worse, have not begun. The project manager's task is to determine not only why the project is under budget, but also why it is behind schedule and what the impacts to the project are.

Some practitioners use CPI and SPI together to obtain worst- and best-case budget estimates at completion. That is, the CPI alone will provide the best-case estimate. The product of multiplying CPI and SPI provides the worst case, since multiplying two fractions yields a smaller fraction and includes the schedule impact. To demonstrate, multiply our CPI of 1.25 and SPI of 0.83 to obtain 1.04 (rounded to the nearest 100th). Then calculate a new LRE as follows.

$$LRE = BAC/1.04$$

or $\quad$ $$LRE = 20,000/1.04$$

$$LRE = \$19,230.77$$

Hence, the new budget estimate falls within the range of approximately $16,000 and $19,000. In actuality, the new estimate at completion for the budget will probably not be as good as the $15,000, nor as bad as the $19,000, but rather something in between, depending on how well the schedule recovers with project management intervention.

One final calculation is important in the earned value analysis process, and that is the estimate to complete.

Estimate to Complete

ETC provides the project manager with an estimate of the amount of money required from a point in time to the estimated end of the project. This figure is important for two reasons. First, the project manager has to know how much additional funding may be required. If nothing can be done to improve the budget picture, then either the customer must agree to additional funding, or the organization must absorb the loss. Naturally, the project manager will endeavor to get the project back on track, but knowing how badly the project is faring will provide insight into what actions need to be taken for recovery. The second reason ETC is important is that the financial organization needs the information for planning future cash flow requirements.

The ETC is calculated by subtracting the actual amount expended on the project from the latest budget estimate at completion. Mathematically, ETC is calculated by this equation:

$$ETC = LRE - AC$$

or

$$ETC = 16,000 - 3,000$$

$$ETC = \$13,000$$

Exhibit 2-11 is a useful table of the most important earned value formulas and their definitions. Exhibit 2-12 is a graphical depiction of the earned value analysis.

Term	Definition	Formula
PV	Planned value of the work scheduled or the estimated cost of each task or project.	PV for project = Total budgeted cost for each of the project tasks. PV for a task is total task budget.
AC	Actual cost to accomplish the work. Money expended to accomplish the EV.	AC = Total of all actual costs (labor, materials, vendor, and subcontractor costs) at time of status checkpoint.
EV	The budgeted amount "earned" or completed against the planned amount.	EV = (% of tasks completed) × PV of project or task as appropriate.
CV	Cost Variance. The difference between the amount earned, that is EV, and the actual expenditures, AC.	CV = EV − AC
SV	Schedule Variance. The difference between the amount accomplished or earned, EV, and PV, the amount planned.	SV = EV − PV
CPI	Cost Performance Index. A measure of the amount earned per each dollar expended.	CPI = EV/AC
SPI	Schedule Performance Index. A measure of the physical work accomplished per each dollar expended.	SPI = EV/PV
SAC	Schedule At Completion. The total project schedule duration.	SAC = Total project schedule

BAC	Budget At Completion. The total project cost.	BAC = Total project cost
ETC	Estimate To Complete. The amount of money needed to finish the project from the point of each status checkpoint.	ETC = BAC (or LRE) − AC
LRE	Latest Revised Estimate. The most recent budget estimate for total project cost.	LRE = BAC (or previous LRE)/CPI
LRS	Latest Revised Schedule. The most recent total project duration estimate.	LRS = SAC (or previous LRS)/SPI

Exhibit 2-11. Earned value terms, definitions, and formulas.

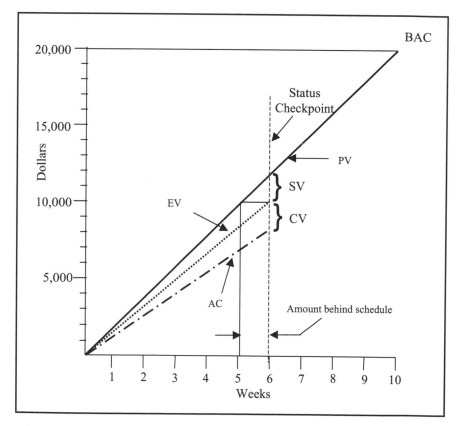

Exhibit 2-12. Earned value graph.

Summary

The vast majority of all information technology projects fail, principally because organizations cannot adapt their management and support processes to the rapid change of technology. These projects also fail because companies don't have the expertise to develop themselves into project-oriented organizations, and, therefore, are unable to put into place the project management techniques and tools required to effectively and efficiently manage IT projects.

There are many project management tools, but the most important four are:

1. The work breakdown structure (WBS)
2. The network analysis
3. The Gantt chart
4. The earned value analysis

Of these four, the most important is the WBS, because with a complete and accurate WBS, the project manager can develop every other tool she needs.

Chapter 3

Information Technology Project and Systems Life Cycles: Project Management and Team Activities

Basic project management tools and techniques are the same regardless of whether one is involved with hardware, software, services, or in an IT project that combines them all. To successfully plan, implement, and complete a project, work breakdown structures, schedules, risk analyses, and other commonly used tools of the trade are needed. The tools are the same—but the projects are different.

Different projects require different technical and management approaches. The application of traditional project management tools and techniques is generally less successful in the IT industry. This is not because these techniques are inapplicable but rather because the unique characteristics of IT projects are not taken into account. In other words, we apply the tools assuming that IT projects have the same characteristics as engineering or construction projects and expect them to respond in the same way. Therein, lies the problem—IT characteristics such as risks, schedule requirements, customer needs, market-driven pressures, and even the competitive environment differ from those found in the traditional project world. So the challenge is not to learn unique tools and techniques but to learn how to apply the traditional ones in a different environment. To do that, we have to understand the uniqueness of IT projects and their products.

A project has both a life cycle and a systems development life cycle during which a number of typical activities occur. The key to planning and managing IT projects is to understand these life cycles, how they fit together to accomplish the project and product requirements, and what activities the project manager is responsible for during the entire process. The project life cycle (PLC) encompasses all the activities of the project, while the systems development life cycle (SDLC) is focused on accomplishing the product requirements.

This chapter discusses how the systems development life cycle fits into the project life cycle and the differences between IT projects and traditional engineering or construction projects. Since one of the principal differences between IT projects and others are the risks involved, a comparison of the risk differences is made in this chapter. A more complete discussion of risk and risk management is found in Chapter 7.

Understanding the environment of any project requires a good understanding of its life phases, what occurs during each phase, and what the project manager is required to do to successfully accomplish these phases.

The Project and Systems Development Life Cycles

Project managers have long known that projects have a life cycle much like a biological life cycle. That is, the project starts slowly, builds steadily to a peak resource and activity level, and then rapidly decreases in resources and activity to the closeout point.

There is no standard nomenclature for naming phases. Often, the initiation phase will be called the concept phase. Planning is sometimes called development, monitor and control are often referred to as implementation, and the word *termination* can replace the term *closeout*. The phase names I use in this book are chosen as a convenient way to differentiate between the project and systems life cycles, but you or your organization may use a different set of names. The important point to remember is that the activities, regardless of the phase name, are the same.

The project life cycle shown in Exhibit 3-1 is typical of an IT project. However, different types of projects can and often do have more or fewer phases than these. For example, a research project might have basic research and proof-of-concept phases before the initiation phase. Also, some organizations view certain activities, for example, project selection or customer services, as being life cycle phases, while others do not. Some authorities argue that customer service in particular and system maintenance

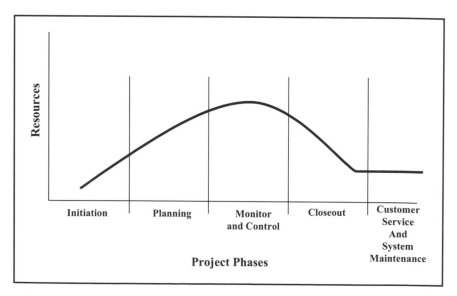

Exhibit 3-1. Typical IT project life.

to a significant degree do not meet the strict definition of a project because these are ongoing activities. However, most IT projects have customer service and maintenance commitments that are contractual, which make them projects. In any event, the long-term customer service and system maintenance activities should be treated as new projects, or as ongoing events. But here, this phase in the life cycle is a legitimate phase because it is the transition between the end of the product development cycle and its following service life.

The SDLC is an underlying or coincident part of the project life cycle. Note that the SDLC is also used in a software development activity to mean software development life cycle, but the term *systems development life cycle* is more appropriate to the IT environment because IT is a systems project, not just a software development project.

Many organizations attempt to manage projects using a SDLC model alone, but neither the project life cycle nor the SDLC is solely sufficient to successfully manage a project; both are required, and it is a serious mistake to ignore either. A close study of Exhibit 3-2 (discussed in the next section) should make it clear why both life cycle models are important to project success.

The Systems Development Life Cycle

Exhibit 3-2 shows the relationship of the project and systems life cycles, along with the typical project manager and project team activities during each of the phases. From this graphic, it should be clear that the project life cycle activities have more to do with planning, administration, and leadership—all those activities necessary to ensure that plans and processes are in place to ensure a smoothly running project. The SDLC activities, on the other hand, are focused on the technical aspects of producing the project deliverables.

Although there is a definite overlap and merging of activities

Project Life Cycle (PLC) Phases	Initiation Phase		Planning Phase		Monitor and Control Phase		Closeout Phase	Customer Service and System Maintenance
Software or Systems Development Life Cycle (SDLC) Phases	Concept	Requirements	Requirements	Design	Implementation	Integration and Test	System Installation	Maintenance or Support
	Project Activities •Gather data •Identify project requirements •Establish project scope •Develop high-level WBS •Estimate resources •Develop charter **Systems Development Activities** •Define product requirements •Develop feasibility analysis •Define product scope •Develop systems architecture		**Project Activities** •Assemble project team •Develop detailed WBS •Develop network analysis •Develop budget and schedule estimates •Write project plan •Kickoff project **Systems Development Activities** •Conduct trade-off analyses •Finalize product requirements •Complete preliminary design		**Project Activities** •Set up project organization •Set up and execute work packages •Direct, monitor, and control project **Systems Development Activities** •Complete preliminary design •Obtain design approval and sign-off •Develop detail designs •Construct system •Conduct unit, system, and integration tests •Deliver system		**Project Activities** •Conduct technical and financial audits •Obtain customer acceptance •Prepare transfer responsibility plan •Evaluate and document results •Close project office **Systems Development Activities** •Install and test system	**Project Activities** •Transfer project responsibility •Develop customer survey plan •Follow-up with customer •Provide customer service and maintain system **Systems Development Activities** •Operate and maintain system

Exhibit 3-2. The project and systems development life cycles and activities.

between the models, it is important that the project manager and his organization realize that the project life cycle encompasses all the activities of the project, whereas the SDLC focuses on the activities of the product. Each of the PLC and SDLC phase activities is explained in more detail below.

Project Life Cycle Activities in the Concept Phase

The first phase of the PLC is the data-gathering phase. The project manager often is not aware of the project until it has been selected and the company is committed to pursuing it. When this happens, there may be very little available information about the project, at least in written form, and the project manager has to scramble to gather as much information as possible in a very short time.

Every project manager has experienced or will experience the scenario described above—a project handed to her with virtually no background or requirements list. When this happens, the only recourse is to find out where or how the project originated and then to question everyone associated with its selection. The objective is to determine why the project was selected, who is for and against the project, the basis of any budgetary and schedule estimates, and what the expected product functions are. If the project was initiated because of a contract award, then much of the needed data can be found within the contract documents or in any proposal that was submitted. In either case, the project manager's job is the same—ferret out the data he needs to develop the project plans.

Project Requirements and Scope

Initially, the project manager must interpret the requirements and plan the project with minimum help because the project team cannot be formed until the level of effort is established. The first task of the project manager, then, is to quickly determine the general scope of the project and the skill sets needed to accomplish the requirements. This task is not as daunting as it seems because, according to her experience, the project manager will quickly develop a sense of the project size and complexity. The requirements will describe the project deliverables or products the customer expects. From this, the project manager can determine the types of skills needed. However, the wise project manager will first determine the general scope of the project and then solicit the help of her peers to develop the details. There are three reasons for this approach.

First, it is always better to have the combined experience and knowledge of a team than to try to know or remember or discover everything alone. Second, as the team members develop an understanding of the project, they will not only have suggestions about the needed skill sets but also specific recommendations about the people in the organization who are best suited to each task. Perhaps the most important reason for using your peers at this stage of project definition is their collective "lessons learned" experience. They will be able to help identify the risk areas in both the customer's stated needs and the organization's ability to respond to them.

The most critical activity in this phase is to identify the customer's requirements. In fact, I have devoted Chapter 4 to a detailed discussion of the subject. At this point, however, it is sufficient to understand that identification of the customer's requirements is vital because it defines not only the product, but also the actions and activities of the project team and the functional organizations supporting the effort. In short, identifying the requirements is the first step in defining the project scope.

Resource Needs

Once the general scope is determined, the project manager can began estimating the number and types of resources needed for the project. It usually is not realistic to have all the requirements identified. As you will see in the next chapter, requirements identification is not particularly difficult, but it does demand careful attention to all the project documentation available, and it requires a disciplined process to ensure that all the requirements are identified. Thus, a general understanding of the project scope is about the best that can be accomplished this early in the project. Of course, the more information that is available on the project, the more detailed the scope definition. For example, if the project results from a bidding action and a contract, then the requirements and the scope will be well understood from the start. It is those projects that are internally generated, no matter how good or important the reason, that typically lack written descriptions or requirements definitions and are, therefore, difficult to scope.

Whether the project is well defined or the project manager is working with a general scope statement, the next order of business is to develop a high-level WBS. Again, the more detailed the requirements, the better the WBS will be. However, remember that the WBS is needed before any final estimates of the types and numbers of resources can be made, or the cost and schedule estimates can be developed.

As with defining the requirements and scope, it is generally better for the project manager to use a team of experienced people to help with developing the WBS. This decreases the likelihood of overlooking a task and increases the speed of getting the WBS completed. In addition, experienced people will have a wealth of lessons learned, knowledge that can aid in determining resources, usually by name. For those project managers who have to negotiate for resources, having the names of the individuals they want when approaching a functional manager is important. The individuals you want may not be available for your project, but presenting the functional manager with the request puts him on notice about the skill levels you need. In other words, it is a good negotiating strategy that often eliminates the problem of having a functional manager provide you with people who just happen to be available and who may not even have the required skill sets. To repeat, using an initial team of experienced colleagues can provide valuable information and save the project from future problems.

This initial team may or may not become part of the project team. In fact, its members often don't become part of the final team because they are likely to be too senior to be assigned task responsibilities. In addition, some of them may be running projects of their own. When the WBS is sufficiently developed to have an accurate view of what the project entails, what resources are required, and, most important, which functional groups in the organization are needed to support the project, then the major output of the concept phase can be developed—the project charter.

The Project Charter

Project charters are extremely important to a project manager's success, and, thus, the success of the project. Yet, most organizations do not prepare project charters. This may be because of a lack of project management training. Or, it may be because these organizations have not embraced project management techniques and concepts as part of their corporate culture. In other words, it is a lack of education on the importance of this tool that likely prohibits its use.

A project charter is not a legal document; it is an internal document that is usually prepared by the project manager and signed by a person who is senior enough to have functional authority over the project and all the supporting functional areas. The primary purpose of the project charter is to name the project manager and to give him the authority to initiate the project. Many organizations will argue that they already have project charters because they send out an announcement each time a project begins. But the charter is more than just an initiation announcement; it is also a commitment to support the project. Each functional manager who is expected to supply resources to the project should sign the charter document. The charter is an excellent way of getting senior buy-in before the project begins.

The project charter usually is short—not more than three pages and often only one page long. The format varies from company to company, but generally it contains a brief scope statement describing the project, how the project supports the strategic goals of the company, who the project manager is, and finally, if possible, the project's priority within the company. The priority is the single most difficult thing to obtain because most companies view all their projects as having the same priority—number one. So even if you do manage to get a project charter written and signed, it is unlikely that you will have a priority assigned to it. However, if you can get a priority assigned, your life as a project manager will be a lot easier when you negotiate for resources. Exhibit 3-3 shows a sample project charter format that can be adapted to any organization in any industry.

I.   Purpose (Scope statement)

II.   Project Establishment (Business reason for the project and how it supports the company's strategic goals)

III.   Project Manager Designation and Authority (Names the project manager and provides the range and limit of his or her authority)

IV.   Project Team Organization (Describes where the project team is within the organizational hierarchy)

V.   Project Manager's Reporting Chain

VI.   Project Organization and Structure

VII.   Project Team Composition

VIII.   Support Organizations and Support Requirements (Describes which functional groups are required to support the project)

IX.   Special Communication Requirements (Used if special reports or unique reporting data or cycles are necessary)

X.   Appendixes (Some companies attach a more detailed scope statement to the charter than is usually given in the Purpose, above)

Exhibit 3-3. A sample project charter outline.

Systems Development Life Cycle Activities in the Concept Phase

The SDLC activities in this phase overlap significantly with those of the project life cycle, which may be why some organizations try to use the SDLC to manage their projects—the overlapping activities give a false sense of doing everything that needs to be done to manage the project. But there also are some different activities as well. In both models, this is the data-gathering phase—trying to get a handle on what the project is all about and, in the case of the SDLC, what the product is.

Product Requirements

It is important to realize that in project management we deal with two scopes: the project scope and the product scope. Whereas the project scope is general in that it addresses all those activities required to support developing the product—the reason for the project—the product scope is very specific and focuses only on the product (or service). The basis of the product scope, as with the project scope, is its requirements.

The challenge in requirements identification is understanding what the customer wants. Generally, requirements are poorly written or incomplete, or the customer simply does not know what he wants. Even when the requirements seem clear and straightforward, the wise project manager will restate them back to the customer to ensure they both understand the direction the product definition is taking.

Product requirements are best stated in terms of functionality desired. Functional requirements relieve the customer of the burden of developing detailed specifications, and it makes describing her product needs easier. Likewise, functional requirements free the provider to develop creative, and usually more cost-effective, solutions. Again, this subject is treated in detail in the next chapter.

Once the product requirements are identified and verified with the customer, the next step in the SDLC is the feasibility analysis.

The Feasibility Analysis

A major problem in any project, but particularly in the IT industry, is that too few organizations actually do a feasibility analysis of the requirements to determine whether they have the resources or technical capability to meet the customer's needs. All too often, the organization simply takes the position that "we can do any project" with no consideration about whether they have the right amount of expertise.

A recent Government Accounting Office (GAO) study revealed that every contract they reviewed failed, or was late and over budget, if the providing organization did not map the customer's requirements against the provider's capability *before* design approval. A feasibility study is crucial to the success of a project, and it should be a part of the requirements identification and high-level WBS development.

Feasibility studies demonstrate to a prospective project owner or investor that a given concept is financially viable and whether further study and/or a business plan is warranted.

For a feasibility study, basic data is obtained from the client through a series of queries, questions, and meetings, wherein the client provides some of the research. Other data and facts need to be gained from a variety of sources.

The typical feasibility study contains, among other items, notes on financial projections, a general description of the business, general details describing how the company/project will be formed, managed, and marketed, statements concerning the competition, and a cash-flow projection based on averages. Further notes can be included as to general details of the project and revelations discovered during the research stage. The study will normally be completed quickly, and it will be presented in a very general format (unlike a business plan). A feasibility study should answer five questions:

1. Will it work?
2. Do we have the expertise and resources to do it?
3. Will it benefit the company?
4. What will it cost to start?
5. Does it fit into the company's strategic plan?

The feasibility analysis serves several purposes. Not only does it help to determine whether the company has the technical and resource capabilities to do the project, but perhaps more important, it answers the question of whether the project would contribute to the company's long-term growth plans. If the project doesn't fit the strategic plan, then whether or not there is sufficient expertise and resources is a moot point—the project should not be started. One further major benefit of a feasibility analysis is that it helps identify and reduce business risks. Technical risks, to some degree, can also be identified by the feasibility analysis, but a more thorough risk assessment is done when the systems architecture is developed.

If the feasibility analysis indicates that the project does fit the company's strategic goals but reveals shortcomings in the provider's capability or resource pool, then the opportunity exists to either hire additional capability, contract with a consultant, or team with another company. Another legitimate strategy is to negotiate with the customer to reduce the product scope, or at least postpone some of the options until the company can develop the requisite capability.

With the feasibility analysis completed, the product scope can be definitized. Product scope is simply the amalgamation of the requirements identification and feasibility study into a statement of product definition.

Product Scope

Product scope can be defined as the features and functions that characterize a product or service. With the requirements definition completed and a well-researched feasibility analysis in hand, the scope of the work to design, develop, and implement the product is well under way.

The product scope is different from the project scope in that the emphasis here is on defining the functions and characteristics of the product and the technical considerations for building it. This is not the process of actually designing the product but defining the parameters within which the product is likely to be built. In other words, the product scope defines the boundaries around the product (i.e., how big, what color, how responsive, and how reliable it is), but it does not dictate a solution. In fact, a good product scope definition won't even suggest a technical approach: It will just specify the product's minimum functionality and characteristics. The technical approach is determined by developing the systems architecture, which determines the product specifications.

Systems Architecture

The National Aeronautics and Space Administration (NASA) defines a systems architecture as:

> ... How functions are grouped together and interact with each other. The architecture applies to the mission and to inter- and intra-system, segment, element, and subsystem.[1]

In other words, the architecture includes every aspect of the system. And "system" is the keyword when defining the IT project. All too often, the emphasis is on the software development component, with the rest of the system being designed almost as an afterthought.

The key elements of architectural design are:

- ✔ Requirements
- ✔ Functional design of alternatives
- ✔ Analysis of alternatives
- ✔ Evaluation criteria
- ✔ Formulation of a preferred system architecture

The architectural design process then is one of identifying the requirements and developing several technical alternative solutions to meeting the customer's needs. The obvious reason for this approach is to determine the most efficient and cost-effective solution. Once the analysis of these alternatives yields the preferred solution, then it is important to establish evaluation criteria to measure whether the alternative is indeed the proper one and how well it meets the requirements.

The architectural design process ultimately results in the formulation of a preferred architecture, which means a detailed analysis and description or specification of the system. With the preferred architecture identified, the serious project and product planning can begin.

Project Life Cycle Activities in the Planning Phase

Many of the activities in this phase will have been started in the concept phase and, perhaps, even completed, depending on how well the customer's requirements are stated. But generally, this is the phase during which project plans and project team composition is refined and finalized. The first task during this phase is to complete and assemble the project team.

The Project Team

Resource requirements are determined from the requirement definition exercise and the high-level WBS development. The earlier the team is assembled, the better, but how fast this activity can be accomplished is purely a function of how well the project requirements are stated and understood from the beginning. It usually takes longer to assemble the team for projects that are generated from within the organization because of the lack of detailed and well-stated requirements. On the other hand, projects that result from competitive bids are better defined. Consequently, it is easier to establish minimum skill and experience levels for them. In fact, some customers, particularly from the public sector, often attach a key personnel clause to the contract, which specifies the minimum skill and experience qualifications the key members of the team must possess. The key personnel requirements, incidentally, become a part of the evaluation criteria when the customer is deciding who the bid winner will be.

Once the team is assembled, their first task should be to finish development of the WBS, because it is the tool upon which all the rest of the project planning depends.

The Detailed Work Breakdown Structure

The WBS may only require some refinements. As with every other aspect of the project at this stage of development, however, the completeness of the WBS is a function of how well stated the requirements are. But with most projects, the best that can be expected at this point is a high-level WBS. The team should finish its development. Even if the project manager and her peers have managed a rather detailed treatment of the WBS, it should be reviewed once more by the team, project manager, and the customer to ensure that all tasks have been captured. Remember, if it is not in the WBS, it is not in the project.

The WBS is the single most important tool in the project

manager's arsenal because it is the basis of everything the project team will do for the remainder of the project. Without it, or without a complete one, good budget and schedule estimates cannot be developed, executable and achievable plans cannot be written, and there will be no accurate baseline against which to measure the project's progress.

It is important that the entire project team be involved in this final push to complete the WBS to ensure completeness and accuracy. This effort also serves as the first team buy-in and team-building opportunity. Finally, the customer should always approve the WBS because it is the instrument that captures all the requirements as well as the supporting project activities. If the customer decides that he does not want to pursue any part of the project, as a result of seeing the effort described by task, then now is the time to make adjustments in the project direction.

The next project team activity is the network analysis, which must be accomplished before budget and schedule estimates can be developed.

The Network Analysis

The network analysis is a tool that is basic to determining the schedule and, consequently, the cost of a project. Incredibly, many project teams and organizations do not do a network analysis: They just make an estimate at the schedule and build their project plans around that estimate. Without a network analysis, it is not possible to optimize the schedule, nor is it possible to identify points of resource conflict that may cause delays in the schedule. If everyone clearly understood its uses, no one would attempt a project without a complete network analysis.

The network analysis has several functions. First of all, it graphically shows all the task dependencies in a project or even in smaller components, such as a phase. The network should be constructed using task-level activities. If it is constructed at a higher level, say at the summary level, it will not reveal the source of problems, should they exist. Second, the network analysis is often the first opportunity to identify risk areas, such as resource conflicts or task dependencies, that might contribute to schedule delays if one or more of the tasks are late. Third, the network analysis identifies the critical path, which is the shortest duration that the project can be accomplished. The critical path, furthermore, defines the project schedule. From the network analysis, the project schedules can be developed.

Project Schedules

Project schedules are estimated from the network analysis, and, in fact, are basically a bar chart depiction of the network itself. It is crucial to develop as accurate a schedule as possible because the other key elements for project success—budget estimation and resource allocation—are dependent on it.

The project can have several schedules. If the project is a large and complex one, the project manager will need a master schedule that provides an overview of the project milestones. The master schedule is particularly important for communicating with the stakeholders and for providing general progress updates. The project manager will also need a schedule that shows each task so that actual progress can be tracked. In addition, the Gantt chart can be used to show milestones, meetings, deliverable dates, and any other information that assists the management process.

The reason that an accurate schedule is important is not so much because of the necessity of accurate progress tracking, although that is certainly important, but rather because there is no way to develop a reasonably accurate budget without it. Hence, the sequence is clear: network analysis to determine the critical path and other task dependencies, schedules by which the progress of each task, deliverable, milestone, and any other requirement can be monitored, and the budget for every aspect of the project. Once these key elements of the project are determined, the project plan can be written.

The Project Plan

The project plan is in some ways a misnomer because it implies one simple, straightforward document. The fact is, the project plan is neither simple nor straightforward. To be sure, there are templates from which a plan can be developed, and there are even software programs that aid in the writing of such plans. But although each plan should have pretty much the same parts, every project, being unique and different, will have to be described in a way that reflects its unique nature. So there really is no way to reduce the project to a routine activity. If that were possible, then project management would be simply an administrative function. Furthermore, the project plan is an amalgamation of several plans. That is, the project plan consists of the general description of how the project will be accomplished, and it also contains all the other plans necessary to support the project.

A key project management activity is the kickoff meeting. Ideally, the project kickoff occurs after the project team has completed defining the project to a significant degree, but that almost never happens.

The Kickoff Meeting

When is the best time to have a kickoff meeting? The right time is when there is enough information available to make the meeting meaningful, informative, and when most, if not all, the stakeholders can attend. This "right" time needs to be early in the project life cycle, ideally at the end of the concept phase or the beginning of the planning phase. However, the tendency is to schedule a kickoff meeting immediately after project approval. Often the pressure to schedule the meeting early comes from senior management because a meeting gives an appearance of activity that the planning function just cannot provide. Having the kickoff meeting too soon, though, can be counterproductive.

The problem with having a kickoff meeting too soon is that

it defeats the purpose of the meeting. A kickoff meeting is an opportunity to provide a statement of the project's scope and general schedules, an indication of the most likely technical approach, an approximation of the resources needed, and an introduction of the stakeholders to the team members. But often the team is well into the planning phase before enough information about the project and project deliverables is available or clear enough to warrant discussing them at a kickoff meeting. However, waiting too late to have the meeting is just as dangerous as having the meeting too early.

Some organizations insist that the kickoff meeting should not be conducted until all the detailed planning is completed. Their rationale is that until the details are known, the project cannot be discussed with any authority. The problem with this kind of thinking is that by the time all the detailed planning is completed, the meeting is no longer a kickoff to the project—it becomes a status meeting. In addition, one of the primary purposes of a kickoff meeting is to get buy-in from the stakeholders.

The project manager and the project team are busy during the planning phase putting the finishing touches on the plans that will ensure project success. Key to developing these plans is the final product architecture.

Systems Development Life Cycle Activities in the Planning Phase

The activities of the SDLC during the planning phase are focused on defining the product alternative selection and, at least, the preliminary design features. Ideally, the activities of the concept phase will have yielded a general understanding and agreement about what the systems architecture will look like. But the final decision about the technical approach is done during the planning phase. One of the key considerations is the trade-off analysis, which reveals the most economic and feasible technical approach.

The Trade-Off Analysis

A critical element of project definition, schedule, and cost estimating is in the consideration of different technical approaches. Although a trade-off analysis can be performed anytime during the project's life cycle, it is most often done during the early stages of requirement definition.

The trade-off analysis is done in conjunction with the technical or functional experts, and it is usually the responsibility of the project manager to decide which approach is the best. The trade-off analysis is used to determine which approach is the most efficient and effective in meeting the customer's requirements. The selection parameters can vary widely. The parameters selected, though, should relate directly to the problem statement. For instance, the problem might be to design an IT system that performs with a prespecified degree of effectiveness and at a minimum life cycle cost. Therefore, the parameters to consider will pertain to system effectiveness and cost. On the other hand, there may be a need to evaluate different off-the-shelf components. In this case, the primary considerations might be supportability, interchangeability, or mean time between failures. The problem will dictate the parameters, and the project manager is responsible for ensuring that the different alternatives are assessed against the proper parameters.

Generally, there are two classes of evaluation parameters: cost and system effectiveness. Obviously, the schedule will be dictated by cost and system effectiveness and vice versa. Within each of these two classes, there are a number of different parameters. Each parameter will be more or less important depending on the customer and the customer's needs. For example, if the project is to deliver a piece of equipment for the Department of Defense, operational necessity and speed of implementation may be the driving criteria, and cost may be inconsequential. Usually, the customer will indicate the criteria that are most important. In that event, these criteria should be a part of the evaluation of technical alternatives. Otherwise, the project manager must determine the criteria she thinks are important, based on what is known of the customer and the customer's stated requirements, and apply a weighting factor to each of the criteria as they are applied in the alternative selection evaluation. Exhibit 3-4 provides a list of parameters that are commonly considered, and it shows an order of evaluation parameters, as the system is decomposed into subsystems and the details of subsystems. Note that Exhibit 3-4 lists no first-order parameters. Usually, we consider system costs to be the first-order parameter because that is the single most important parameter in any project. Even if the overall cost is not the princi-

TECHNICAL ALTERNATIVE EVALUATION PARAMETERS

Second-Order Parameter	• System effectiveness	• Life-cycle cost
Third-Order Parameter	• System performance • Operational availability • Dependability • Capacity for growth	• Research and development costs • Investment costs • Operation and support costs • Phase-out costs
Fourth-Order Parameter	• Accuracy • Range • Size and weight • Reliability and maintainability • Speed • Supportability • Transportability	• Design costs • Data cost • Test and evaluation costs • Manufacturing costs • Inventory costs • Maintenance costs
Fifth-Order Parameter	• Accessibility • Diagnostic aids • Handling • Interchangeability • Logistics requirements • Producibility • Operator skills • Safety • Storage • Utilities • Test requirements	

Exhibit 3-4. System alternative evaluation parameters.

pal evaluation criteria in determining contract award, cost is the ultimate discriminator because the customer will have a budget cap. Also, in evaluating technical approaches, the efficiency of a system is measured, in part, against its cost-effectiveness.

The problem is to select the best approach possible through an iterative process of system analysis. This process is demonstrated in Exhibit 3-5. The process can be very time-consuming and, in some cases, very subjective. One of the major problems for many project managers or project team members is that they often forget the ripple effect of changes in a system. That is, each time a change is made to a system or each time a new alternative is considered, a sensitivity analysis is required to determine the overall effect to the system.

A process for managing project time, cost, and performance trade-offs should emphasize the systems approach to management. To manage this trade-off process, the following steps should be taken:

- ✔ Identify the basis for project conflict or possible redirection.
- ✔ Review the project objectives and requirements.
- ✔ Analyze the project status.
- ✔ Identify any alternative courses of action.
- ✔ Analyze and select the best alternative.
- ✔ Document the actions taken.
- ✔ Revise the project plan.

The objective of performing a trade-off analysis is to find an alternative course of action. A good approach to trade-off analysis is to identify several courses of action by brainstorming with the project team and other functional experts. With several approaches identified, the best approach, in terms of an efficient technical solution and costs, can be determined.

It is important to remember that each alternative must be weighed against the project requirements and objectives. A good

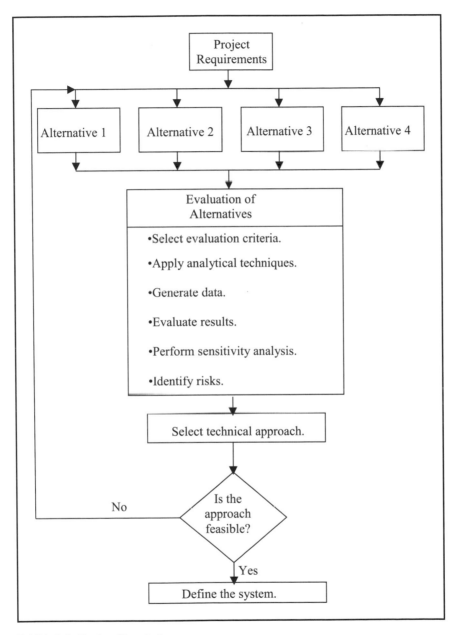

Exhibit 3-5. Trade-off analysis process.

technical approach is not always the most cost-effective one or the best in terms of schedule. Every change or potential change has a ripple effect throughout the system, and sensitivity analyses must be performed.

Exhibit 3-5 shows that several alternatives are analyzed before the best one is selected. In fact, all the alternatives must be analyzed and tested for their sensitivity to the system before the best one can be chosen. That is why the trade-off analysis process is such a time-consuming one. But because this process is so time-consuming, it is often skipped, often with disastrous results.

Once the trade-off analysis is completed and all the stakeholders agree upon the best technical approach, then the product requirements can be finalized.

Finalizing Product Requirements

It should be obvious by now that the process of defining requirements, both for that project and the product, is iterative in nature. That is, analyzing what you think the customer wants and verifying it requires open and active communication channels. With the proper attention on developing a comprehensive WBS and rechecking that the systems architecture definition still accurately reflects the customer's needs, the product requirements can be fleshed out and the product requirements list and/or specifications can be finalized. It is at this point that it will be clear, both to your organization and to the customer, that the project is achievable or not and that the product can be designed with the requested functionality or with any approved changes in the scope.

The next step in this phase of the SDLC is to complete the preliminary design.

The Preliminary Design

In our model of Exhibit 3-2, this step is listed as "complete preliminary design." You will notice that there is no "start preliminary design" step because the preliminary design has been evolving from the requirements analysis, feasibility studies, systems architecture development, and trade-off analysis. In fact, the preliminary design should be pretty much completed by this point except for any refinements necessitated by finalizing the WBS and product requirements. In other words, the final touches can now be put to the design and to any plans that need updating. The next step in the process is to obtain stakeholder and especially customer approval so that the detailed design can be developed.

Design Approval and Sign-Off

Design approval and sign-off by the customer and other key stakeholders is critical to a successful project. One of the major reasons for project failure in the IT industry is that this key step is often bypassed in deference to getting on with the coding. The thought seems to be that the design will naturally evolve as the code is written—it won't. It could, if the only component of the project were to design software. But the preliminary design must include the system—that is, software, hardware, communications, training, and whatever other product component—and it must include the integration of all of these elements. So this design thing is not trivial; it is the heart of the project.

Develop Detailed Designs

The phrase "Develop detailed designs" is very descriptive of the activity—it means to develop to the greatest detail possible the design for each component of the product, its construction, integration, test, and final delivery. This element of the system development cycle often includes several critical milestones set by the customer. Even if the customer doesn't require specific design review checkpoints, it is a good idea for the project manager to have the customer review them. The reason for these reviews is to ensure adherence to the design parameters, but just as important, it is the best way to assess the viability of the technical approach. What seemed like a good idea in theory may prove unworkable once the pieces are put together.

Once the design is complete, and again, approved, the construction of the product can begin in earnest.

Constructing the System

It would seem that an inordinate amount of time has passed between the point of project go-ahead and the start of constructing the product. Relatively speaking, there has been a considerable amount of time spent in the planning and designing stages. And this is the very thing that makes many senior managers, as well as project managers, nervous—spending time planning and designing when they could be "coding like hell." The problem is that the planning/designing functions do not have the "feel" of making progress, whereas the action involved in coding or building does. Hence, the tendency is to skip right to the actual building cycle. As hard as it may be to do, the project manager *must* resist the temptation to shortchange the planning and design cycles, and she *must*, to the best extent possible, resist senior management's urgings to get on with it. It is not unusual for world-class organizations to spend half their project's budget before the project is actually implemented, that is, engaging in the build, test, and install phases. As Dwight D. Eisenhower said, "The plan is worthless; the planning is priceless."

So it is with IT projects. If the right amount of planning and design work has been accomplished, the construction of each of the project components can now progress—usually with little or no snags. Bear in mind that, in an IT project, there will be at least two components and probably three or four that have to be built, and some or all of these components will need building parallel to meeting the schedule. This concept will be explored more fully in Chapter 9.

Unit, System, and Integration Tests

Testing in any project, and especially in IT projects, is often one place where significant delays can occur. The delays are not usually the fault of the testers, although they can be, but rather because testing organizations often have a limited number of available, highly skilled testers on staff. If the organization typically has several projects running at the same time, then scheduling the test window is critical. The wise project manager will factor this potential schedule problem into her project plan and ensure that "begin testing" is one milestone that is met.

Testing project products is a project within itself. The essential steps in the testing phase are:

✔ Write a test plan incorporating functional requirements and features of the product(s).

✔ Develop a test suite based on the test plan so that all the product functions and features are tested individually, as subsystems where appropriate, and as an integrated and complete system.

✔ Execute the test suite and report any discrepancies from the plan. Resolve discrepancies as bugs, test case errors, or deficiencies, as appropriate.

✔ After discrepancies are corrected, prepare the final product for release and installation. Archive all product documentation and test components.

It is important to note that there usually are three different tests run on the product—the tests on individual components, tests on subsystems, and tests on the integrated final product. These tests don't include ongoing software code testing. So the testing function is not only critical to the overall quality of the finished product, but is one that can be in and of itself an intensive and sometimes grueling endeavor. To skimp on the testing, though, is asking for trouble when the system is delivered to the customer.

Delivering the System

The delivered system is the culmination of the project's technical effort and represents the reality of the customer's stated needs and requirements. The system with all its components is the final act of both the SDLC and the PLC. It is why the project was initiated.

The delivered system may be physically delivered to a customer site or, if the customer is internal to the organization, it may simply be delivered by powering it up. Regardless of whether the customer is internal or external, the process should be treated the same—as if delivery is the conclusion of a written contract. Otherwise, there will be problems with the final phase of the project life and systems development life cycles.

Project Life Cycle Activities in the Termination Phase

The activities in this phase are basically administrative for the project manager. She has to ensure the project requirements have all been met and that the customer agrees that the product is acceptable. This phase is often the most difficult phase of a project. The pressure is on to finish the work and meet the budget, schedule, and performance goals set at the beginning of the project. But because of the nature of business, the functional managers supporting your project need those resources for beginning other projects. The project manager often finds himself trying to keep enough of the team together to complete the work that is left. Without completing these termination activities, the project could continue unfinished for months or even years.

Technical and Financial Audits

There are two audits that are absolutely required before closing the project. They are the technical audit and the financial audit.

The technical audit is performed to determine whether the requirements of the project have been completely met. The project manager and team accomplish this audit by reviewing the scope and specification documents and comparing the requirements against the WBS. If all the requirements are met and the final project deliverables are completed, then the technical audit can be successfully closed.

The financial audit is precisely what one would expect it to be an evaluation of the finances to ensure that all vendors are paid and that all invoices to the customer are prepared and submitted. The financial audit also compares the actual costs against the planned cost of the project to determine how closely the initial estimates were. This part of the audit becomes extremely important in one of the other termination activities—evaluating and documenting the lessons learned.

Once the audits are completed, the very important step of obtaining customer acceptance can be accomplished.

Obtaining Customer Acceptance

Project managers, and organizations in general, often make the serious mistake of not ensuring that the original contract or internal memorandum of understanding, if not covered by contract, contains a completion criterion for the project. Completion criteria are established so that the customer can state clearly what the provider must do to satisfy the terms of the agreed project parameters. Completion criteria protect both the customer and the provider because they each know precisely what is expected of the other. Without these criteria, the customer can always claim that the provider has not met the project requirements, and the project will never be closed. Generally speaking, this is not a scenario that is often played out because the customer wants the project finished as much as, if not more than, the provider.

Getting customer sign-off on the project officially completes the project, but there are still activities that have to be finished.

Preparing a Transfer Responsibility Plan

In most cases, IT projects are transferred to another organizational group or team for care and maintenance. The actual maintenance of an IT system is not a project but rather becomes a functional activity. Nevertheless, all the documentation and work of the original project can be viewed as the statement of work (SOW) or scope for the maintenance phase. So the closeout of the project should be accomplished with this view in mind. The successful maintenance and continued customer satisfaction of the product depends in large part on the quality of the information handed over to the maintenance team. Hence, a thorough and well-documented, supported transfer plan is a major activity during the project termination; this is yet another reason for holding the team together until *all* phase activities are completed.

Evaluating and Documenting Results

One of the most neglected activities of the termination phase is the "lessons learned" effort. The reason so few organizations support this activity is simply that there is a rush to start the next project, and the resources are desperately needed elsewhere. In short, the feeling is that the organization can't afford to lose its resources to this kind of activity. The irony is that a lessons learned meeting generally only takes two to three hours because most of the data are already available in the status reports. Basically all that remains is to collect individual thoughts, opinions, and comments about what went well and what didn't during the project. It is also important for the project manager to record his evaluations of the project team members. The objective in a lessons learned exercise is not to place blame but to evaluate actions and skills, people and technical skills, so that future project teams have the benefit of knowing how best to utilize the talents of the resource pool.

After the lessons learned activity is completed, the only thing left is for the project manager and team to close the project office.

Closing the Project Office

Closing a project office is difficult or relatively easy, depending on whether the office is a loose structure within the organization or an actual office on the customer's site. If the latter, there can actually be a considerable amount of work involved. There may be a rental agreement that has to be paid off or terminated. Or, a transfer of responsibility has to be made. There also may be utilities and telephones to disconnect, and office furniture that must be disposed of. In many instances, the customer will have furnished equipment, usually computers, for the development effort. If so, these customer-owned assets have to be properly accounted for, returned, or disposed of in accordance with the client's direction.

In addition to disposing of the physical assets of the project office, the project manager is responsible for archiving the project documentation. This documentation usually is of two types: the project control book, which contains all the plans, status reports, and all other technical information, and the legal documentation. The legal documentation will contain such things as the contract, if from an outside customer, or a memorandum of understanding, if from an internal customer. It may also include memoranda between the project manager and customer and other stakeholders, in addition to any other documentation that has to do with the contractual aspects of the project.

One final but very important project manager activity in this phase is the reassignment of people resources. The project manager may not have functional responsibility for the team members. In fact, she probably won't have that responsibility unless the project operates in a projectized organizational structure. But at the very least, the project manager should make recommendations about how best to utilize the team members. This action not only engenders trust and loyalty on future projects. It also helps the organization maximize the use of individual skill sets.

Systems Development Life Cycle Activities in the Termination Phase

The SDLC activities of this phase are not necessarily simple, but they are straightforward—install the system and make sure it runs as advertised.

Usually, installation of an IT system is fairly simple, if the components have been built according to the plan and if they have been thoroughly tested. In fact, the integration tests will have required that the components all are connected and working together, so the system has already been installed once. Still, the proof of the pudding is in demonstrating that the system works as the customer expects. So, although this is the only activity in the SDLC for this phase, it is actually the crucial one, because if it doesn't work as the customer expects it to work, then it may be back to the drawing board.

Once the system is installed, the provider tests it to ensure it functions as expected. In addition, the customer is likely to have had a contract clause specifying that he be allowed to operate the system to determine its functionality and adherence to the stated requirements. In fact, this often is the test of acceptability by the customer. Only upon the successful conclusion of this test is the system accepted. But once it is accepted, the whole project is completed and closed. Now a new phase of customer relationship begins—operation and maintenance of the system and continued customer satisfaction.

Project Life Cycle Activities in the Customer Service and System Maintenance Phase

This area is not, traditionally, a phase of the project life cycle, nor is it an SDLC phase. However, it is my belief that it should be a phase of both cycles. In reality, the follow-on maintenance and customer service functions occur here. However, the tendency is to treat these activities as separate from the original project. In one sense they *are* separate—the project of developing and delivering the product *is* complete. But in a very real sense the project is never over while the customer is using, and expecting good service from, the product. Thus, it is logical that we consider follow-on activities as part of our project responsibilities.

The customer service and maintenance functions do not fit the definition of a project. That is, they don't have a defined end date, unless there is one dictated by contract. But the work of the project—training materials, manuals, operating procedures, specifications, and so on—serves as the SOW (statement of work) for those who are responsible for maintaining the system and ensuring the customer is satisfied with how the product operates. This SOW should be transferred to the maintenance/customer service team by formally passing the responsibility from the project team to a service team.

Transferring Project Responsibility

A memorandum of understanding should be used to transfer the project responsibility, regardless of whether it is for an internal or external customer. Once the project is installed and tested to be operationally ready, the project team is essentially through with the project work, except for the remaining administrative details. But unless the system continues to function in a manner pleasing to the customer, the effort has been wasted. Therefore, it is crucial that a smooth transfer from the project team to the maintenance and customer service teams (usually these functions are separate) be made. It is best to have in place a formal transfer procedure that includes training on and about the system for those who will continue the customer interface. In addition, it is my recommendation that the project manager of the original project contact the customer two to three months after the product is installed to inquire about how well the system is functioning. This inquiry serves two purposes; first, it gives the customer time to operate the system and to determine whether it truly meets all the stated requirements. Second, it demonstrates to the customer that the provider is sincerely interested in providing quality products.

Developing Customer Survey Plans, Following Up with the Customer, and Providing Customer Service and System Maintenance

Every organization should prepare good customer survey plans. This subject is discussed more fully in Chapter 12. Surveying customers about products you have provided is the fastest way to determine whether your project management processes are adequate. Customer surveys, and occasional visits to the customer, are the best ways to follow up with the customer.

    The sole objective of this phase of the project life cycle is to maintain the product and to ensure that the customer is satisfied with the work your organization has done in providing the IT product of her dreams.

Systems Development Life Cycle Activities in the Customer Service and System Maintenance Phase

The SDLC activities in this phase are focused on one thing only—maintaining the system.

    Too many organizations do not differentiate this activity from the project. This is particularly true in IT efforts for internal customers. That is, the thinking is that the project continues as long as the system is in place. The problem with this approach is that there is never any closure from one activity to another. It is important to the project manager and the team members to have a sense of accomplishment. I have already stated that the maintenance and customer service activities are not truly projects in the traditional sense, and they are not. But these activities should be appended to the project and systems development life cycle so that the relationship between the project and the follow-on responsibilities is clear. And there should be a definite and distinct demarcation between the project and follow-on efforts.

Summary

There are two distinct life cycles at work in a project—the project life cycle, which encompasses all the project work including the systems development, and the systems development life cycle, which focuses on the product or products of the project. Many organizations make the mistake of trying to manage their project using only the SDLC. It is a mistake to assume that either the PLC or the SDLC is sufficient by itself—both are needed to successfully manage any project, but particularly one as complex as any IT project.

The PLC and the SDLC models have overlapping activities. It is not possible to completely separate the two any more than it is possible to delineate between the phases of either model. But thinking of the models as having distinct phase activities is helpful in understanding what the project manager and his team have to do in order to successfully complete the project on time, within budget, and to the customer's performance specifications.

Note

1. National Aeronautics and Space Administration, NASA Engineering Management Council, *The NASA Mission Design Process* (Washington, D.C., 1992).

Chapter 4

Identifying and Developing Customer Requirements

More than half of the errors in a project originate with the requirements and analysis activities done before product design. The opportunity to eliminate these largest error contributors is ignored in most organizations, and particularly in those industries with rush-to-market livelihoods. In these industries, the tendency is to begin coding, or constructing the product, or building the system as soon as possible and to depend on defining or refining the requirements as the project progresses. This approach may, or may not, produce a product within the available market window. Even if it does result in a product, the cost of error repair far outweighs the cost of up-front planning and analysis. Furthermore, error-prone products are poor-quality products, and poor quality is passed on to the customer—it is as simple as that.

I am not suggesting that all projects have completely definable requirements all the time. Many projects, particularly those involving new or cutting-edge technology, may start with only general ideas about the end product's purpose. In these instances, it is appropriate to develop the system requirements as the project progresses. But even under these circumstances, the requirements definition process has to be disciplined, documented, and scrupulously followed. A more detailed discussion about evolving or adaptive requirements methodologies is contained in Chapter 10. However, first it is important to understand what a requirement is and why it is so crucial to project success.

The customer defines requirements. The customer, whether internal to the organization or external, desires a product or a service to meet some need and then communicates this need to the provider. The problem is that the customer often cannot describe precisely what he wants, or the product may be too cutting-edge for the customer to even understand fully its functional capabilities. Or, the customer may know exactly what she wants but may not be able to communicate the requirements clearly. To make matters worse, the producing organization may not have a process for identifying and analyzing requirements and thus may be incapable of correctly interpreting them even when they are clearly communicated.

This chapter defines requirements and their importance to the project management process, the identification and analysis of requirements, and the process required for translating the requirements into a successful project that satisfies, to the greatest extent possible, the customer's needs.

What Are Requirements and Why Do We Need Them?

The customer establishes requirements usually as a result of some operational need—that is, some need the organization has for improving its capability, competitiveness, or dominance in a particular area. Requirements often are the result of the organization's strategic objectives and may be driven by the company's need to improve or change its core business.

A specific requirement is something a product (or service) must do or a quality the product must have. Any requirement exists primarily because the customer wants the product to have the particular functionality or quality. A requirement also can exist simply because the product type demands certain functions or qualities. For example, to be truly functional, a product that is used in testing might need to be self-aligning or self-calibrating to a preset tolerance. Hence, a secondary requirement to self-align is inherent in the product's functional capability because of the primary requirement to test rapidly, often, and accurately.

Most of us can readily accept that a product must have certain functional requirements, but many of us don't realize that there also are nonfunctional requirements. Understanding the different types of requirements is crucial to identifying and planning to meet them.

Functional Requirements

A functional requirement is one that the product must have to provide the capability needed by the ultimate user. Actually, functional requirements are the fundamental basis for the product in the first place. If a product does not provide a function, do a job, or complete a task, then the need for it goes away. An example of a functional requirement statement is:

> **The product shall produce an amended resource availability roster at the end of every work shift.**

This statement says that for the product to be serviceable to the user, it must provide, among other things, the capability or function of keeping track of and reporting on the available resources each time a work shift comes to an end.

Generally, a description provided by the customer will yield several, even hundreds, of functional requirements, depending on the complexity of the product. But for every functional requirement, there also can be one or more nonfunctional requirements.

Nonfunctional Requirements

A nonfunctional requirement is a quality or property that the product must have. Sometimes this type of requirement is critical to the product's success, but often it simply enhances the product's looks or identifies the product as something unique to the organization. Nonetheless, it is a requirement, and it is important to the customer—sometimes even more important than a functional requirement. An example of a nonfunctional requirement statement is:

> The Essex Company logo will be prominently displayed on the front of the product.

This requirement, the company's logo, clearly doesn't affect the functionality of the product. The product will work regardless of whether the logo is present. But to the Essex Company, this logo prominence may be of significant marketing importance, particularly if the product is critical to an operation and its contribution is seen by hundreds of people. Consider, for example, the timing equipment used at the Olympics. As important as the accuracy and reliability of the equipment is, it is just as important, to the provider at least, that the company name be prominently displayed on or with the equipment.

Nonfunctional requirements are often overlooked during the requirements identification process or, if not overlooked, they are considered less important and not given the appropriate attention. This negligence can be catastrophic. Consider the following story.

Several years ago, an elderly woman living in an old Boston mansion decided to sell her house and move to another state to be near her children. The woman, a widow, had lived in the house nearly her entire life. The house was built around the turn of the century by her parents; she grew up in the house, inherited it from her parents, and raised her own family there. But as she aged, she wanted to be near her two children, both of whom lived and worked in Florida. The house went on the market, but the woman rejected every offer, even several that exceeded her $3,000,000 asking price. She finally accepted an offer from a young couple for a little over $2,000,000. When asked why she rejected every offer but this particular one, and for nearly $1,000,000 less than the asking price, she explained her reason. "Every person who made me an offer had grand plans for either changing the house or for demolishing it altogether to make room for a completely new house. The man who offered me the most money even planned to subdivide the property and build several nice but smaller homes. I didn't want to see the house I was born in and lived in my entire life destroyed. The young couple that bought the house told me they didn't have the price I asked, but they loved the house so much they wanted it so they could eventually restore it to its original condition. Furthermore, they promised me that they would not change my bedroom for as long as I live, but would leave it as is for me to visit and use anytime."

This story is not about requirements in the sense that we are considering project descriptions, but it demonstrates an important point. What the customer really wants may not be obvious. Her real interests may be nonfunctional. In the example of the woman and her house, the primary requirement was selling the house so she could move to Florida. But the woman's overriding desire was that the house be preserved in the way that she had cherished it. The moral of this story is that we must be careful to identify and interpret *all* of the customer's requirements.

Project Constraints

One more important consideration in identifying requirements is to realize that some requirements actually represent constraints. These constraints may take the form of constraints to the project process. Or, a constraint may be that the product is in and of itself a constraining device. Either way, this condition may generate other requirements. For instance, if the requirement is for a device to be delivered by a certain date, not unusual in federal sector contracts, then the schedule represents a constraint. This scheduling constraint may force the provider to hire additional personnel or consultants or even to team with another company to meet the deadline. If the product is something that is used in a dangerous environment, then the environment may impose additional requirements. An example might be a product used in a military vehicle, say, in a helicopter or tank. Although the product itself might be rather benign, the very nature of its operational environment will dictate its design parameters. For instance, a computer in a tank must be "ruggedized" to withstand the forces imposed on it by the tank's operational environment.

Remember, all requirements have to be fulfilled to the customer's satisfaction before the project can be considered a success, and some requirements are more important than others. In other words, not precisely meeting the requirement that a product be a certain color to match the company's logo will not affect the functionality of the product, and perhaps it results only in a less than totally satisfied customer. This result is not unimportant, but it is relatively harmless and easy to rectify. But not considering requirements that are also constraints usually results in significant cost and schedule overruns, complete failure of the project, total customer dissatisfaction, or all of these conclusions. Requirements are not only important—they are the very heart of the project's existence. How, then, can we eliminate or at least reduce this significant problem source?

The obvious answer to eliminating problems resulting from requirements interpretation is for the customer to establish clear and concise requirements and for the provider to ensure they are precisely interpreted. Yet how can these actions be brought together to yield the desired result? There are three key steps: a clearly written set of requirements, a medium for transmitting these requirements to the provider, and a process for ensuring that the provider and the customer are in complete agreement about the intent of the project and the results desired. Let's begin by looking at the first step—providing a clearly written set of requirements.

Writing Requirements

Written requirements are expected when the customer is external to the organization. If an organization lives or dies by its ability to bid for contracts, as in the defense industry, it would be inconceivable that written requirements would not be provided in the form of a statement of work (SOW). Yet, when the customer is internal to the organization, it is more likely that a written description of the desired product or service not only won't be provided, but will not even be considered. The fact is, all projects should have written requirements, and each internal project should be viewed and managed just as if it is governed by a binding contract. The reasons for doing this will become clear in the following sections.

The best requirements writing guides are the requirements or specification documents from previous, successfully completed projects. The organization's lessons learned archives quickly yield the basic elements for developing a working template for writing your next project SOW. Some tips for describing your requirements and developing a good SOW are shown in Exhibit 4-1.

Writing a good SOW—that is, developing a project requirement statement—is an art and the ultimate test of good written communications skills. A requirement should be written in as simple language as possible and should be stated in one sentence. If you find that describing a requirement takes more than one sentence or requires two or more verbs and/or conjunctions, then you are probably describing two or more requirements. Consider this requirement statement:

> The product shall be capable of testing 300 samples per hour and shall print test results on a standard-size sheet (8½ by 11 inches) in a two-column, tabular format.

There are actually two requirements in this statement. The first deals with how many samples the product must test per hour.

- **Describe the work**—Describe all the work to be done as completely, clearly, and concisely as possible.
- **Do not dictate how to do the work**—Write a functional description of the desired product or service when possible.
- **Clearly differentiate requirements**—Describe only one requirement per requirement statement.
- **Avoid ambiguous statements and words**—Avoid words or phrases that do not have exact meanings.
- **Repeat the statement of requirements for clarity and legality**—If requirements are embedded in other documents attached to the contract, repeat them in the statement of work (SOW) or include them by reference.
- **Include illustrations, tables, charts, and diagrams**—Include anything in the SOW that aids in understanding the requirements.
- **Flow down requirements**—Pass on my requirements from prime contracts to subcontracts. Requirements imposed on the prime provider by the customer must be included in the vendor's SOW for the vendor's area of work responsibility.
- **Always have the statement of work reviewed/critiqued by others**—A review by an objective reader will reveal how clearly the SOW is written.

Exhibit 4-1. Tips for writing good statements of work.

The second addresses the test report characteristics. The point to be learned here is that whether writing or interpreting requirements, it is important they be completely differentiated to avoid overlooking one or more of them.

We have discussed that the customer develops and writes his requirements as a part of the statement of work, but we have not yet discussed precisely what this document is. The statement of work is the second step in bringing the customer and the provider to an understanding of the project's purpose. In short, the SOW is how the requirements are transmitted to the provider. It basically defines the project scope and is the communication medium in the process of defining the project.

The Statement of Work

Statements of work are most often associated with requests for proposals (RFPs), which are the formal documents issued by a buying organization inviting potential vendors to bid on a contract. However, organizations need to practice writing SOWs for their internal projects as well. As we shall see, the SOW is a definitive description of the work, and having such a document can only aid the project team to fulfill the desires of the customer, whether internal or external.

There are several reasons a SOW is critical to project success. First, this is the document that completely describes the work to be done. Second, the SOW describes what constitutes acceptance. That is, the SOW should always contain a section that describes what the project team must do to provide an acceptable product or service, and, likewise, how the customer will measure project completion. Unless this completion criteria is explicitly stated in the SOW, the project may never reach a conclusion because the customer can always claim the deliverable did not meet her intended desires or needs. Third, the SOW takes precedence over all other documents. For instance, if a specification attached to the SOW describes the desired functionality of the product differently than the statement of work describes it, the SOW is the document that must be followed. Of course, the discrepancy between the two documents should be pointed out to the customer for clarification and possible amendment. Many providers have assumed that, for instance, the engineering specification describing the product is precisely what has to be delivered. They later found themselves redoing the product, at company expense, because the SOW described something slightly different.

For smaller, less costly projects, the buyer might issue a specification or needs statement. The difference between this statement and the SOW is in the amount of detail included. However, whatever term is used, the goal is the same—to describe the needs of the customer. In this book, we will concentrate on the SOW because that is the most difficult and most detailed of the needs descriptions. But even statements of work can take on a different focus or include a different amount of detail depending on the form they take.

Types of Statements of Work

There are three major types of SOWs. They can be based on:

- ✔ Design or detailed specifications
- ✔ Level of effort
- ✔ Performance

Although there are other types and variations of each of these SOWs, these generally meet the needs of most IT projects.

Design or Detailed Specification Statements of Work

Design and detailed specification statements of work tell the provider how to do the work. They may include precise measurements, tolerances, materials, quality control requirements, and any other specific constraints determined to be important to the customer. There are definite advantages and disadvantages to this type of SOW. Some of the advantages are:

- ✔ The customer is able to describe precisely what she wants and how it is to be built.

✔ There generally is less potential for misinterpreting the customer's requirements.

✔ The provider is relieved of bearing the risk for the project.

✔ Up-front efforts are generally reduced. That is, there generally is less design required or less testing required of various technical solutions.

The disadvantages of this type of SOW are:

✔ The customer must bear the major risk burden in the project because he is dictating the solution and how it is to be provided.

✔ The customer may not get the most cost-effective or most functional product since this approach precludes evaluation of other solutions.

✔ It generally produces poor projects in the IT world because it dampens, or even eliminates, creativity.

This SOW is often used in the manufacturing or construction business, but other work efforts are often described in this format. It can be used to good effect in the IT environment, but should be used with discrimination and only for small, highly defined projects. Otherwise, the very essence of IT, namely creativity, is compromised.

An excellent type of SOW that is used effectively in practically any type of service industry or project is the level-of-effort SOW.

Level-of-Effort Statements of Work

Level-of-effort (LOE) SOWs can be written for almost any type of service unless it is an inherent organizational service. The real deliverable under this type of effort is an hour of work. That is, the customer contracts for time and pays the provider according to the amount of time spent providing the task. Usually, this type of contract has a weekly or monthly cap on the amount of compensated work, which requires the provider to closely control the amount of scheduled work. The provider generally has to produce proof, in the form of certified time sheets, to the customer before payment is made. This type of SOW can also be used within an organization to track how much effort is expended in accomplishing such projects as upgrades to managerial systems control processes.

The most efficient and effective SOW model is, however, the performance-based statement of work.

Performance-Based Statements of Work

Performance-based statements of work are always the preferred method for transmitting the customer's needs because they structure all aspects of an acquisition around the purpose of the work and not around how to accomplish the work. This approach has a number of advantages to both the customer and to the provider. The two most important advantages are that the provider or contractor has the freedom to develop and evaluate different solutions to meet the customer's requirements. The customer can concentrate on obtaining the desired provider instead of the provider's processes. This approach usually costs less than the design or detailed specification SOW because the focus is on functionality rather than on meeting precise engineering measurements. That is, it is generally more important that a desired result is obtained from turning a knob than it is that the knob be turned precisely one-quarter turn to obtain the result. The cost of engineering the latter example is significantly higher than designing for functionality.

It is possible that some combination of SOW types may be needed. For example, an IT project that addresses a satellite communication system must of necessity contain specifications describing close engineering tolerances. Likewise, satellite size and weight constraints are described in the SOW and accompanying documents, but many of the other project requirements are described in terms of the functions the system must perform.

Statements of work, being the most essential documents in any solicitation, contract, or important internal project initiative, must be written so that all technical and nontechnical readers can understand them. But writing good SOWs is not easy. It requires close attention to detail and a thorough understanding of the customer's needs.

The investment of time and effort to write a clear and high-quality SOW:

✔ Enables vendors or internal project teams to understand clearly the customer's requirements and needs.

✔ Allows project teams to more accurately schedule and cost the effort and to develop a higher-quality technical solution to meet the requirements.

✔ Minimizes the need for change orders or other project adjustments, which can increase project costs and, usually, schedule durations.

✔ Provides a milieu for establishing performance and completion criteria.

✔ Allows both the customer and the project team a way to assess performance and progress.

✔ Reduces claims and disputes.

There are several SOW format variations that are effective and useful, but generally all SOWs have the same basic sections. A general format is provided in Exhibit 4-2, and the content of each of its sections is described in the next several paragraphs.

The Statement of Work Format

The statement of work can be thought of as the project specification. As such, SOWs typically describe the technical aspects of the

Statement of Work

I. Scope
II. Background
III. Applicable documents
    a. Specifications
    b. Standards
    c. Industry/organizational documents
    d. Other documents
IV. Requirements
    a. General
    b. Detailed project requirements
        i. Systems engineering
        ii. Systems analysis and control
        iii. Baseline generation
        iv. Software design
        v. Hardware design
        vi. Training design
        vii. Delivery and installation
        viii. Concept of operations
        ix. Maintenance/customer support
        x. Design reviews
            1. System requirements review
            2. System design review
    c. Program management
        i. Program management system
        ii. Risk assessment, mitigation, and management program
        iii. Life cycle cost (LCC) analysis and control
    d. Program electronic database
V. Acceptance criteria
    a. General guidelines
    b. Buyer's measure of acceptability
        i. Product demonstration milestones
        ii. Test/review requirements
    c. Provider's responsibility for demonstrating product acceptability
VI. Reporting requirements
    a. Review meetings
    b. Status reports

Exhibit 4-2. A statement of work format.

project. Other important subjects such as background, applicable documents, and acceptance criteria reporting requirements, or any other pertinent contractual requirements not discussed in the SOW, are addressed in the project plan. Although many SOWs will contain engineering specifications, usually as attachments or appendixes, many will not, nor should they. This is especially true of SOWs that have been prepared as performance-based documents. Yet thinking of the SOW as a specification gives an added emphasis to the importance of the document, if there is still any doubt. This thinking also helps focus the writer's attention on providing clear and concise descriptions of the work, and it helps focus the reader on the salient points of the document. Each of the SOW sections is briefly described below.

✔ *Scope.* The scope section is really an introduction to the project. In one sense, it is a little misleading because we think of the SOW as providing the project scope. Thus, it is logical to assume that this section would do exactly that. However, this section is simply a high-level statement of what is described in the rest of the SOW and generally what the project is about. An example of the scope section is:

> This statement of work defines the effort required for the design, engineering development, software programming, fabrication, and test of a prototype of the (project name) information technology system to determine system feasibility. It includes the associated project management, human engineering, and logistics support planning requirements.

The Exhibit 4-2 statement of work format may be more comprehensive than you need for your project, particularly if the project is relatively small and without the usual complexities of most IT projects. If that is the case, use the applicable sections of the format and skip the others. Likewise, add any sections not in the format that are important to your project's success. Remember that every project is unique, so providing a format that fits every situation is difficult if not impossible.

The focus thus far in this chapter has been primarily from the viewpoint of the customer. Understanding what requirements are, how they are developed by the customer, and how they are transmitted to the provider is essential to understanding the next step—interpreting statements of work and identifying the requirements.

Identifying Project Requirements

Generally, identifying project requirements is not difficult; it just needs careful scrutiny of the statement of work and/or other project documents, such as the contract, specifications, and any correspondence leading up to project initiation. That is not to say that it's a small task. The larger the project, the larger, usually, is this task of identifying the requirements. Still, the task is not difficult if there is a disciplined process in place.

The Requirements Identification Process

Defense industry companies generally have well-defined requirements identification processes because their survival is directly dependent on their ability to successfully bid on and win contracts. Other companies, public or private, that depend on bidding for business also know how to identify and interpret customer requirements. However, most companies and organizations typically have a very difficult time identifying their customers' requirements and often don't even realize the need for it. The following process should help you if your organization doesn't have one in place.

Every company may approach requirements identification in a slightly different way, but the basic process is essentially the same regardless of the industry and regardless of whether the customer is internal or external. The four steps in this process are:

1. Determine whether the project is one that should be pursued.
2. Look for special conditions placed by the customer.
3. Capture all the requirements in every document pertaining to the project.
4. Develop a matrix that cross-references each requirement to where it is found and where it is addressed by the project plan.

Although I have listed only four steps in this process, each of the steps has multiple substeps. These steps are addressed in detail in the next several sections.

Determining Whether to Pursue a Project

Many companies assign people or even a department to be responsible for determining whether a project, internal or external, is one that should be pursued. This would seem to be an obvious thing to do, but the fact is, there are just as many companies that do not have any kind of a formal review process, and, therefore, find themselves in the middle of a project that should never have been started.

Bid or project review generally is accomplished by an ad hoc committee constituted specifically for the purpose. This committee sits in review as the need arises. Exhibit 4-3 presents a checklist for considering whether to bid on an external solicitation. It should be obvious that the checklist is equally applicable, with minor alteration, for determining the viability of pursuing a project that develops within the organization.

The first two questions in the checklist deal with examining the solicitation or project in light of the company's core business and whether the project will improve the company's market share

_____ 1. Is the project consistent with our core business?

_____ 2. Will the project meet or further our corporate goals?

_____ 3. What experience gaps do we have in the organization?

_____ 4. What technical gaps do we have in the organization?

_____ 5. What personnel gaps do we have in the organization?

_____ 6. What do we know about the customer/stakeholders?

_____ 7. What does the customer know about us?

_____ 8. Would a team member (another organization or company) improve our chances of winning the contract (successfully completing the project) by enhancing our internal capability or improving our credibility with the customer?

_____ 9. Should our company be the prime contractor or a subcontractor?

_____ 10. Who is our competition?

_____ 11. What are the competition's strengths and weaknesses?

_____ 12. Do we have the resources to meet this project's requirements?

_____ 13. What is the probability of winning the contract or starting the project?

_____ 14. What is the probability of successfully completing the project?

_____ 15. What is the start-up cost of this project (writing the proposal and gearing up to initiate the project)?

Exhibit 4-3. A checklist for making a bid/no-bid decision.

or meet other corporate goals. Many companies chase contracts or projects that appear achievable or that are offered by customers that they think they know, believing that these factors provide enough advantage. They discover too late that they do not have the requisite expertise and experience—it is not a part of their core business. Even if an upcoming project is within the core business, it does not mean that the project would further the company's goals. If, for example, the company is targeting projects with opportunities to enhance its technical capability, then the project should be under the core business umbrella but with elements that enhance its expertise.

Questions three, four, and five in Exhibit 4-3 focus attention on the current internal capability to perform the project. Before embarking on a bid for any contract, or before pursuing any project, it is necessary to understand if there are any existing gaps in the company's capability to perform. If so, then alternatives need to be developed to allow the company to pursue the project (i.e., if the responses to questions one and two are positive).

Questions six and seven are more difficult to quantify than the previous five questions because they deal with perceptions. A company can be confident that its marketing department has made all possible efforts to get to know a customer and vice versa. However, whether the customer really knows or likes the company remains questionable unless they share previous contracting experience. If the company has not done work for that customer before, then the question becomes, "Do we have time to educate the customer about us?" Often the answer to that question is no, unless it is known that the project will not be initiated for a least a year; less if the customer is internal to the organization.

Otherwise, questions eight and ninc of the checklist become very important. Note that these two questions, which deal with the possibility of teaming with one or more companies, support questions three, four, and five as well. In other words, if there are technical, experiential, or personnel gaps within the company, the chances of a contract win, or a successful project, improve by teaming with companies or organizations that can fill those gaps. Likewise, teaming with a company that has a long, positive history with a customer is one of the best and quickest ways to become known to the customer.

Questions ten and eleven deal with a competitive analysis. All the likely bidders should be known, along with their relationship to and experience with the customer. If the competitive analysis reveals that your company is likely to be the highest bidder, all the other questions in Exhibit 4-3 become moot. Finally, if all the other questions can be answered in a positive way and the cost of initiating the project is within company guidelines, then the project should be pursued. Otherwise, the project should be avoided regardless of how attractive it appears on the surface.

Once it is decided a project will be pursued, then the serious work of identifying the requirement details begins.

Special Customer Conditions

Almost all projects have specific conditions that have to be met in addition to the usual project/product requirements. These conditions are easily identified because the customer will draw attention to them even when he is lax in their description of the project's general requirements. The most common special conditions, some of which are actually constraints, are:

- ✔ Scheduling conditions
- ✔ Reporting cycles and types of information expected
- ✔ Budget conditions
- ✔ Environmental standards
- ✔ Developmental and quality standards
- ✔ Exclusions from participating in follow-on contracts

It is not uncommon for the project completion date to be dictated, and that is understandable since the project is in place to address a need, and usually that need has to be met by or before a specific date. For instance, in information technology and other highly competitive industries, there almost always is a window of opportunity for the product to be on the market. If the window of opportunity is missed, then the value of the project is zero or at least greatly diminished.

Many customers, in particular those in the federal sector, dictate the number and types of reports, reviews, inspections, and meetings that they expect. In addition, they also will specify the kind and depth of information to be presented and the frequency of these events. In the private sector, such requirements exist, but usually they are less stringent and often are left to the provider to determine.

The budget for a project also can be a limiting factor, particularly if the customer has not performed a good estimate of the cost to perform the project. Frequently, many projects begin with inadequate funding.

Standards of all types are usually a part of any formal solicitation. Even internal customers provide guidance about how the product will be assessed. In addition, many industries have standards that are imposed on them by regulating agencies, developmental practices, and financial institutions. All the pertinent standards are listed in a formal solicitation, and they should be identified and listed for an internal project as well.

Occasionally there are specific instructions to the provider that if the project is undertaken, then the company will be barred from performing any follow-on projects that evolve from the given project. An example of such an occurrence would be a project that is done to determine the requirements and specifications for another project. A company that develops these requirements and specifications would have a decided advantage over any other company if the customer issued a solicitation for the follow-on work. Hence, the customer will usually bar the original provider from bidding so that the competition is fair. This, however, is not something that happens very often in the private sector and especially not in the information technology industry.

The special conditions or requirements are, as I stated previously, generally not difficult to spot because they tend to jump out at you, and they are usually highlighted by the customer. In fact, it is common, if there is formal project documentation, for the customer to include a paragraph with the heading for special conditions. But ferreting out all the other requirements can be a challenge unless you follow some simple guidelines.

Capturing All the Project Requirements

If identifying requirements is difficult, it is because one must read every line of every document that is provided about the project.

The good news is that 99 percent of the requirements are contained in the SOW. The problem is that some projects, because of their complexity or the sheer size of the effort, have other documents such as specifications, the contract, engineering drawings, and other explanatory material associated with the solicitation. There are two key things to remember if you are involved in such a project. First, the SOW is the governing document. Any other document is subservient. So if there is, say, a specification attached to the SOW, and the specification describes the product's size or function differently than the SOW, contractually the SOW is the guiding document. Of course, the wise project manager will clarify the discrepancy; however, don't make the mistake of thinking that the specification, because it is a more detailed description of the product, is the correct version. Second, although the SOW is the primary or guiding document when resolving discrepancies, it is not the only document containing requirements. The requirements search must be carried throughout all existing project documentation.

Formal Solicitations

In a formal solicitation, the requirements search is actually simplified because all requirements are introduced with a "shall" clause. That is, the SOW or other documents state that "The provider shall build . . ." or "The product shall be capable of . . ." So identifying requirements begins by finding and listing all such statements. Incidentally, if the customer intends to provide equipment, data, special tools, or anything else to support the project, she identifies these items by introducing them with a "will" clause in such formal solicitations. For example, "The buyer will provide to the contractor data to support . . ." or "The buyer will provide computers for . . ." So it is equally important to identify what the customer brings to the project because that affects how the project is planned and how the schedule and costs are estimated.

Internal or Informal Projects

It is far more difficult to determine project requirements for those projects that are internal to the organization than it is for formal solicitations because, typically, there is little or no documentation to describe the product. Early in this chapter, I pointed out that every project should have a SOW describing precisely what is to be accomplished in the effort. But the general feeling among many organizations is that if a project is internal, there is no need for a formal SOW. Perhaps there is no need for a SOW as formal as is found in a solicitation, but at the minimum there needs to be a scope statement describing the product, the customer's requirements, special items such as schedule and budget, and the criteria for project completion.

Once all the requirements are identified and listed, then the most important step in the process occurs—creating a cross-referencing matrix.

Cross-Referencing Requirements Matrix

The cross-referencing requirements matrix is a useful tool for mapping the requirements against where they are found—that is, in the SOW, specifications, drawings, and so on—and against where they are addressed in the work breakdown structure. Exhibit 4-4 is a sample requirements matrix that demonstrates how this tool is developed. Please note that it is only a partial matrix of a fictitious project. A complete matrix can be several pages long.

This matrix serves several useful purposes for the project manager. First, it serves as a worksheet for identifying the requirements. Just having the form in front of you helps you focus on the task of identifying all the requirements, and, in this capacity, it is a constant reminder that requirements exist in all relevant project documents. Second, many of the same requirements will be addressed in different documents. Hence, the cross-referencing action allows the project team not only to determine which documents discuss the same requirement but whether the description in each is the same. If not, then the customer needs to be notified and asked for clarification. Nevertheless, remember that until or unless the inconsistency is clarified, the statement of work is the

Requirements	SOW	Spec	Drawing	WBS
Provide a distributed IT infrastructure for the ATLAS project	Para 1, Scope Definition	Intro		2.3.2 Dist. IT Infrastructure
Develop a grid communication system to support the ATLAS	Para 6.b, Section C		Plate 3	2.3.2.1 Design & model grid architecture
Integrate all the ATLAS software services	Para 3 c, Section E			2.3.2.2 Integrate grid software services
Develop a data management system	Para 14 & 15, Section G		Plate 6, 7	2.3.3 Grid data management
Integrate database tools to management of ultralarge databases	Para 4 g.2 Section B			2.3.3.1 Integrate database tools
Develop, integrate, and test tools and middleware infrastructure to support and manage Petabyte-scale information volumes		Para 13 & 25		2.3.3.2 Build middleware infrastructure

Exhibit 4-4. A sample requirements matrix.

guiding document. Third, the cross-referencing document provides a way of ensuring that each requirement is addressed in the WBS. If it is not in the WBS, then it is not in the project.

Identifying requirements should not be drudgery. It is not difficult, but it does require attention to detail, and it requires that every document initiating the project be thoroughly reviewed. Unless all the requirements are identified before the planning begins, then the project can suffer delays, additional costs, and even failure.

Summary

Requirements are the reasons for projects. The customer has a need that she wants to satisfy and provides the project team with requirements to satisfy that need. It is the function of the project manager and the team to correctly identify all requirements of the project and to provide a plan that, when implemented, will satisfy each of the requirements.

The most important document that customers use to transmit requirements is the statement of work. The SOW is always provided in a formal solicitation, but not usually for an internal project. However, organizations need to make the SOW a part of their operating policies. Lacking that, the project manager, when he is assigned a project, should prepare an SOW outlining the project scope, as he understands it. Then he should get the customer's endorsement before the project is initiated.

Identifying requirements is not difficult when well-written project documentation is available. It does, however, require attention to detail and a thorough review of all the documentation. An important and very useful tool in identifying all the project requirements is the cross-referencing matrix. This matrix helps identify the requirements and provides a way of referencing each requirement to each relevant project document. This way, if the requirement is referred to in more than one document, the descriptions will be consistent. Finally, and perhaps most important, each requirement can be referenced to the WBS to ensure that the requirement is specifically addressed in the project plan.

Poorly written or misinterpreted requirements are the biggest cause of project failure. Properly identifying the customer's requirements, whether the customer is external or internal to the organization, and developing and executing a strong project plan to address these requirements are the major functions of the project manager and her team.

Chapter 5

Organizing the Project Team

In today's environment of intense competition, rapidly changing technology, fluid organizations, and highly complex projects, organizations need highly trained project managers if they have any hope of success. Most organizations acknowledge the need for better-trained personnel. Too often, however, training expenditures are approved only for the technical-based competencies. This practice is particularly prevalent in the information technology industry or any industry that is heavily dependent on high-tech competencies.

Selecting the Project Manager

If selecting the right project to meet an organization's strategic goals is the most important decision senior management makes, then the next most important decision is choosing the right project manager. Just because a person has been a project team member on several projects, or just because the person has been a successful functional manager, doesn't mean she will be a qualified project manager. Project managers require specific skills and knowledge in addition to the general skills and knowledge characteristic of functional managers. The good news is, these skills and this knowledge can be taught. Even so, not everyone will excel as a project manager; only those who are able to apply the skills and knowledge will be successful.

Over the past twenty years, it has become clear that certain characteristics are absolutely crucial for success as a project manager. These same characteristics are sought by organizations when project managers are hired and selected to run their plans.

Characteristics of the Successful Project Manager

To some degree, it is unfortunate that those who run projects are referred to as managers because there is so much involved in being a truly excellent project manager.

Almost all project literature will list the following as, at least, the core and most important characteristics of a project manager:

✔ Leadership
✔ Communication skills
✔ Negotiating skills
✔ Problem-solving skills
✔ Ability to influence the organization
✔ Credibility
✔ Ethical behavior

Leadership

The traditional view of management and leadership is that management is concerned with efficiently and effectively using a company's resources to accomplish the company's business, while leadership is more concerned with innovation, challenging the status quo, and broadening the company's outlook and capabilities. Managers try to get people to agree about the things that need to be done. As Warren Bennis and Burt Nannus (professors at the University of Southern California) so succinctly describe the difference between managers and leaders; "Managers are people who do things right and leaders are people who do the right thing."[1]

Project managers have three basic responsibilities in managing a project: to be on or under budget, to be on or ahead of schedule, and to meet the customer's performance criteria. So it makes sense that project managers must have management skills to accomplish the project's goals successfully. But management skills without leadership skills are very likely to lead to poor results or even failure.

An in-depth study identified a number of characteristics important in a leader.[2] The top four characteristics were: honesty, competence, the ability to look forward, and inspiration.

Communication Skills

Communication skills are important for any manager. For the project manager, they are absolutely critical. When one considers the amount of time a project manager spends communicating with his team, the project sponsor, stakeholders, and senior managers throughout the organization, it becomes readily apparent that a poor communicator has almost no chance of completing the project as planned. The project manager requires not only excellent speaking skills, but writing skills as well. This is because a large percentage of communication is in the form of reports. When I think of how important communication skills are in project management, I am often reminded of a classmate who, when he discovered that he was required to take a speech class, exclaimed that he was studying to be an engineer, not a speaker. In today's business world, there are very few professions in which success does not depend on how well the practitioner communicates.

Negotiating Skills

Negotiating skills rank closely with communications skills in importance, and indeed one cannot be a successful negotiator without possessing excellent communication skills.

Project managers are constantly faced with issues relating to scope, cost, and schedule objectives, organizational objectives relative to the project goals, changes to the scope, resource assignment and allocation, and team conflicts.

Many project managers also are involved in contract negotiations. If a project is the result of an external contract, it is not unusual for the project manager to have been a part of the negotiation team. Likewise, the project manager usually is a part of the negotiation team when hiring vendors, or when teaming with other companies to pursue a project.

Problem-Solving Skills

Problem solving is more than evaluating a problem and determining a solution; it also involves making a decision.

Project problems can be the result of technical incompatibilities or even the lack of a technical capability. They can be interpersonal in nature or they could result from functional managers reassigning one or more of the resources. They also can take the form of external difficulties with environmental or other regulating agencies. Whatever the source, it is the project manager's responsibility to assess the problem and determine the best course of action to resolve it. Finding a solution to a problem, though, is only half the job. A decision about how or even whether to implement the solution must be made.

Decision making usually involves investigating several options and choosing the best solution for the problem and the good of the project.

Ability to Influence the Organization

Most people avoid using the word *politics* when speaking of their job. The fact is, though, that polishing and exercising one's political skill is crucial to success, especially in dealing with stakeholders. The project manager's influence in an organization can be fragile at best, but exercising his political skill is one way to build influence.

In his book on project management, J. Davidson Frame defines a three-step process that a good project politician follows:[3]

1. *Assess the environment.* The environment of the organization is determined by the corporate culture, so the project manager must be sensitive to the corporate goals and strategies and who the relevant stakeholders are.

2. *Identify the goals of the principal actors.* Making sure the project goals are consistent with those of the stakeholders is the surest way a project manager can obtain and keep them as allies. To understand a stakeholder's goals means asking: "What drives this person? Does she have a hidden agenda? If so, how can I deal with this hidden agenda?"

3. *Assess your own capabilities.* Successful project managers know their own strengths and weaknesses and how best to capitalize on their strengths. Once the project manager identifies the stakeholders and their goals, he has to act to mitigate any negative feelings or reservations about supporting the project.

These three steps—assessing the environment, identifying the goals, and assessing your own capabilities—are the basis of increasing political awareness about the culture in the organization, and is one way to increase your influence in the company.

Credibility

Credibility means that the project manager is known to be a person of integrity, knowledgeable, capable, and dependable. A reputation for credibility is earned; it cannot be established overnight, and it will not be believed until it is demonstrated. This quality is something that the project manager must work at with patience and persistence. The only way to be credible is to deliver as promised, be honest in all dealings, and be consistent in behavior.

Almost every other mistake a person makes can be overcome and forgiven—but not dishonesty. Once a person lies, no one fully trusts her again, and her credibility disappears.

Ethical Behavior

Ethical behavior has become so important in project management that the Project Management Institute (PMI) requires every PMI member to sign a Project Management Code of Ethics. In fact, one of the surest and fastest ways for a Project Management Professional (PMP) to lose her certification is to exhibit unethical behavior.

Ethical behavior simply defined means to do what's right. Yet, many professional project managers will risk damaging their credibility and violate their ethics rather than admit that they are having a problem with a project. This is a serious failing.

A major problem, though, is that the project manager is sometimes caught in the difficult situation of being directed by a senior manager not to reveal a problem to a customer. The rationale is that the problem will be corrected without the customer's ever being the wiser. In this situation, you have to evaluate your ethical code and decide whether your conscience will allow the lie, and if you are willing to risk your professional reputation.

Certainly some judgment is required about the seriousness of a problem and whether it is a breach of ethics not to inform the customer. Every project suffers daily snags, irritations, and false starts. The customer will not be interested in these problems—they are the normal difficulties encountered in running a project. However, if the problem is severe enough to cause a delay or requires a short-term infusion of additional resources, the customer needs to know about it. The customer will not be upset that the project encounters a problem, but she will be very upset to learn of the problem after it is so big that there is a significant impact on the project. Customers typically accept problems as long as they can be a part of the solution.

Emotional Intelligence

If not high-tech competencies, what should project managers be learning along with project management tools and techniques?

High IQ or High EQ?

The information technology industry has put a premium on intelligence, and it is easy to understand why. Technology changes so rapidly that developers and users must have the mental capacity to envision new and better ways of using products even as they develop and manage them. Consequently, the most important characteristic for a new hire is a high intelligence quotient (IQ). At least that is how the industry viewed it in the early years of the information technology explosion. But as surviving IT companies become more stable and organized, they are learning that IQ, although important, is not the most important or best measure of a good project manager or team member. More important is something called emotional intelligence or emotional quotient (EQ).

Emotional quotient is, loosely defined, the ability of a person to manage his emotions as well as to manage the emotions of others. In 1995, Dr. Daniel Goleman, a psychologist, published the international best-seller, *Emotional Intelligence: Why It Can Matter More Than IQ.* Dr. Goleman brought together years of research to show that EQ matters twice as much as IQ or technical skills in job success. His studies of more than 500 organizations proved that factors such as self-confidence, self-awareness, self-control, commitment, and integrity not only create more successful employees but also more successful companies.

Why Do Emotions Matter?

Cultural wisdom has taught us that the workplace is not the place for emotions. Reason and logic have been our guides most of our lives, and intelligence is what we've honored. But we all know of high school honor student classmates who have never been able to hold a steady job, while the class cut-up became the unlikely success story. That is because IQ is only one measure of performance, and a very limited one at that.

On some level, we have always recognized that the ability to understand, monitor, manage, and capitalize on our emotions can help us make better decisions, cope with stress and project failures, and interact with others more effectively. Now, thanks to research by Dr. Goleman and others, there is hard data to prove it. I have generalized some of the study results below.

✔ Research on different jobs in a variety of industries worldwide showed that abilities vital for success were trustworthiness, adaptability, and a talent for collaboration—all emotional competencies.

✔ Corporations seeking MBAs report that the three most desired capabilities they seek are communication skills, interpersonal skills, and initiative.

✔ The top 10 percent of computer programming performers exceeded average performers in producing effective
programs by over 200 percent, and the superstar performers produce even higher percentages. The reason for this
astounding performance is that high EQ people are better
at teamwork, staying late to finish a project, and mentoring coworkers. In short, they don't compete—they col-
laborate.

✔ People who score highest on EQ measures rise to the top
of corporations. Among other things, these top performers possess more interpersonal skills and confidence than
the average employee.

Defining Emotional Intelligence

Emotional intelligence is much deeper than having good interpersonal skills. It is being aware of and in control of our own emotions while being empathic enough to perceive and manage the
emotions of others. This does not mean controlling others—it
means understanding others' emotions well enough to lead them
to better performance. The competencies of EQ fall into the five
groups shown in Exhibit 5-1. Of the five, self-awareness and self-
management are the key groups and the ones that are seldom
taught as a part of interpersonal skill training. And unlike IQ,
emotional intelligence can be learned. Researchers estimate that
EQ training takes about five days. In one day of training, one can
gain an awareness of what emotional intelligence is and why it
matters. In three days, one can learn specific skills that can be
applied right away. But it takes five days to understand one's own
emotional makeup, learn the necessary skills, practice the new
behaviors, and experience the kind of transformation that impacts
the organization.

Organizations are concerned about hiring project managers
with high IQs and about providing them with high-quality train-

Self-Awareness	• Self-confidence • Emotional self-awareness • Accurate self-assessment
Self-Management	• Self-control • Trustworthiness • Conscientiousness • Flexibility • Goal-oriented
Self-Motivation	• Self-starting • Commitment to improving • Enthusiasm • Persistence
Social Awareness	• Empathy • Organizational awareness • Service orientation
Social Skills	• Mentoring • Leadership • Communication • Change agent • Conflict management • Building bonds • Teamwork and collaboration

Exhibit 5-1. Emotional intelligence competencies.

ing, but the more successful project managers will also possess a high EQ. Not too surprisingly, it is also becoming more apparent that many in the project team hierarchy need to possess higher levels of EQ.

Structuring the Project Team

How to structure the project team has become more of an issue as projects become more high-tech. Before the advent of the IT age, many project team members had only to be skilled in their specialty. Generally, it was left to the team leaders or the project managers to provide any leadership or mentoring to the rest of the team. However, as projects become larger and more complex, the more members of a project team having highly developed interpersonal and emotional skills, the more successful the project. People who possess these skills are mentors and collaborators, not competitors. Hence, a team with members who possess these skills is more close knit, efficient, and effective. Fortunately, these kinds of skills also make different types of teams function more effectively.

Most project managers are familiar with the three basic types of organizational structures: the functional or traditional, the project, and the matrix organizational structures. Of course, there are many variations of these structures as organizations try to capitalize on their different advantages while mitigating their disadvantages. For example, many organizations have come to view the matrix as the most preferable structure. However, some organizations, because of their mission or function, simply cannot survive without an overarching traditional structure. The most notable example of the latter is the Department of Defense (DOD). Because of its mission, a strong traditional structure is absolutely crucial. Yet, because they recognize the benefits of a matrix organization, many organizational entities within the DOD have adopted cross-functional teams to provide the functionality of a matrix organization. Cross-functional teams are teams that are made up of members from different functional units who are brought together to perform a specific project. Although the team members report to a project manager to meet the project's goals, they each remain assigned to their original functional homes. This scheme provides the benefits of a matrix structure without transforming the entire organization.

Another type of organization that has emerged specifically as a result of the IT industry is the virtual team. A virtual team is, simply stated, a team of professionals who pursue shared objectives while based at distant sites. They rely heavily on electronic, i.e., virtual communication media. A virtual team can also be "global" in the literal sense, as well as in a cultural sense. The geographic and cultural diversity of virtual teams offer challenges to management, but even more challenges to the concept of mentoring or providing other EQ benefits to the team. Although virtual teams have become indispensable—more than 80 percent of companies use virtual teams—more than 50 percent of them fail to attain their objectives. Virtual team failures are most often due to breakdowns in members' working relationships, communication, and trust, which are barriers presented by long distances and cultural differences.

To ensure that management and the benefits of EQ are brought to the team, successful virtual companies take a 90/10 approach—90 percent people and 10 percent technology. This approach focuses on people and their needs rather than on the e-mails, teleconferencing, video conferencing, and media technology that supports them. In this way, the objectives for virtual team effectiveness, including the benefits of EQ, can be met. The objectives should strive for:

- ✔ A strong team leader who is committed to team success, not merely his/her own success
- ✔ Team members who are committed to team longevity, and to their own longevity with the team
- ✔ All members that share a strongly felt, publicly avowed commitment to high team performance
- ✔ Each member committing to adapt his or her behavior and style in order to support the team's success
- ✔ A team that explicitly pays attention not only to task issues, but also to relationship issues
- ✔ A leadership, their policies, and the firm culture supporting the team's success

Organizing and developing the virtual team with these objectives in mind, and a project manager who realizes the importance of periodic face-to-face individual and team meetings, will significantly improve not only virtual teams but on-site teams as well. It is especially important to remember that newly formed teams, particularly those tasked with difficult or complex assignments and who must come to consensus by exploring divergent perspectives, need a chance to get acquainted and build the intimacy and trust necessary to progress through the stages of team development.

Staffing the Project Team

Project team staffs can range in size from one person to several thousand people, but the staffing begins with the assignment of one person—the project manager.

In some business environments, notably the federal sector, the project manager is involved in the project from the time of proposal preparation through the end or hand-off of the project to a maintenance team. There are some significant benefits of this approach. A proposal to a federal sector customer is designed so that it constitutes, among other things, a management plan. So when a contract is awarded and the project manager moves from the role of proposal manager to the job of actually managing the project, she will start off with a completed project management plan. Also, by the time a contract is awarded, the project team staffing will have been determined and ready to begin work.

The majority of projects do not have this genesis in the private sector. In most cases, top management makes the decisions. Then, after the project is initiated, management names the project manager. The first task, and one of the most important tasks, of the project manager is selecting—and getting—the personnel needed to accomplish the job.

The project manager often encounters difficulty in getting the right people for the project. Often several projects are competing for the same talent at the same time. In addition, functional managers may be reluctant or even unwilling to make requested personnel available. Furthermore, if a transfer is required for someone to be part of the project team, the requested person may be unwilling to transfer. In this case it may be more cost-effective not to transfer the resource but rather set him up in a virtual office. With all these challenges, how then does one staff the project? The process of picking the required talent is simple enough; the difficulty, as we have seen, is in obtaining the talent.

Identifying the Project Team Members

The process for choosing team members should not be done by the project manager alone. Although at this stage of the project, she is virtually alone in the game, there are ways to identify exactly what skill sets and experience are needed to successfully complete the job.

First, the project manager has to do a high-level assessment of the project requirements. When doing this, it will become obvious what functional groups have to be involved in the task work, and it is likely the assessment will bring to mind similar projects that have already been accomplished within the organization. A survey of the lessons learned library should also provide some ideas about the numbers and types of personnel needed for the project.

Second, after determining generally what types of tasks are required for the project, the project manager can form what I call a core or initial project team. This initial group is not meant to be the working project team, although some of the group could evolve to that team. The initial group is comprised of other project managers, senior task leaders, and supervisory personnel—anyone with experience relevant to the project at hand. The purpose of assembling such a group is basically threefold:

1. A group possessing this level and kind of experience is exactly what the project manager needs to completely define the project requirements

2. Having defined the project requirements, the group can identify the skill sets that are needed.

3. The group will know who in the organization possesses the skill sets and experience needed to assign against the tasks.

Third, knowing who you want for the project and getting that person is the next challenge. To be successful, the most critical skills for the project manager are highly refined negotiation skills with good communication skills a close second. This is because the project manager will, in most instances, be required to negotiate for the personnel he wants for the project. My advice to project managers is to always go to the functional manager and request by name the person you want for the project. You may not get this person because that individual may be otherwise committed. But when you request someone by name, that puts the functional manager on notice about the level of skill competency and experience you expect for the project team. So even if the specific individual is unavailable, the functional manager is more likely to provide a substitute who has equal or better qualifications. If you do not request people by name, the functional manager is likely to provide you with someone who is not working on a project and who also may or may not have the requisite skills and experience you need.

Once the project team members are identified and selected for the project team, the next task is to organize the project structure so that it complements the organization and provides the best structure to accomplish the project requirements.

The Project Organization

The project organization, simply stated, should be an organization that *best* accomplishes the goals of the project.

There are several ways a project team structure can be organized. Again, the best project structure is the structure that maximizes the team and organizational capabilities to accomplish the project goals. Within that framework, the project organization will take one of the following forms:

✔ Individual
✔ Functional
✔ Matrix
✔ Project

In an individual project organization the project consists of only one person—the project manager. It may be that the project only requires one person, such as a technical survey to determine the best software and equipment to use on an upcoming IT initiative. But often we think of an individual project organization as being one where the project manager has project control of the functional people doing the actual project work, but the team members are not 100 percent dedicated to the project. Actually, the project manager, in this case, is better described as a project coordinator.

The functional project organization is one that is embedded within a particular functional group. That is, the project manager is assigned along with functional people in the group to do a project. Although the project manager has project control, he still does not have functional control of the team members. Nevertheless, the team is formally organized along functional lines, and although the team members still may not be 100 percent dedicated to the project, they tend to have more of a personal commitment to the task work. That is, the project has a more defined organizational quality to it than the individual project discussed above. There are many advantages to this type of structure, the most obvious being that any needed expertise is resident within the functional group. But there is also a very significant disadvantage to the structure. When the team is working within its functional group and does not have functional reporting responsibility to the project manager, there is often confusion among the team members about who actually is in charge of the project. This is because there is always the potential for a functional manager to interject herself into the project leadership role and usurp the project manager's authority. When that happens, it usually takes the project manager a few days to get the project stable again, but in the process he has to reestablish his leadership authority.

The matrix organizational structure is one in which the project manager has project control and the team members are assigned to the project from various functional groups. The project manager still does not have functional responsibility for the team members—they report functionally to their own organization—but his authority tends to be better defined. In addition, the team members are even more dedicated (during work) to the project. It is worth noting that many organizations are structured along matrix lines, but even those that are functionally organized (such as a military service branch) often use a cross-functional team concept to enjoy the advantages of the matrix concept.

Perhaps the best organization of all, at least from the project manager's viewpoint, is the project organization. In this type of organization, every team is organized to support a specific project, and every team member is 100 percent dedicated to the project—the team does not work on any other projects. In this concept, every team member reports directly to the project manager both from a project control perspective and a functional perspective. The project manager has complete authority and responsibility for the project. The primary disadvantage of this structure is that it is usually too expensive—many project functions, principally administrative, financial, and legal, could be shared by all the ongoing project initiatives, so there is significant duplication of resources within the total organization.

Of course, it is unlikely that your organization will exactly mirror one of the ones discussed here. It is more likely that it will be a variant of one or even a combination of one or more. It is not usual for you to change your project's organizational structure during the life of the project to suit the needs as they arise. For example, during a proposal effort, the structure is likely to be an individual type where there is a project manager/proposal manager who borrows people from various organizations to develop the proposal. After the contract, perhaps a matrix organization best meets the needs of the team. Then, after delivery of the system, perhaps some type of staff organization with customer and technical services will be sufficient.

When the project organization structure is put into place, it must support the team's efforts to deliver the product/system to the customer's requirements, and it must be one that enables the project manager to manage her stakeholders.

Stakeholder Management

By stakeholder management I mean managing the expectations of all the project stakeholders. Many project managers remark, after a discussion about stakeholders, that they now understand why their project was not completely successful: They had failed to identify the stakeholders. And, if they had identified them, they failed to meet their expectations or to keep them properly informed about the project.

Stakeholder management involves a number of interconnected activities. These activities must be accomplished and managed while the work of the project progresses. Exhibit 5-2 is a model of the stakeholder management process and how it fits into the project management environment. These steps or activities are discussed in some detail below. However, before we get into how to manage stakeholders, it is important to define exactly what a stakeholder is.

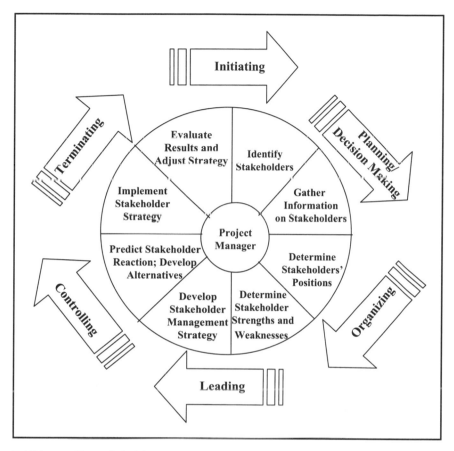

Exhibit 5-2. The stakeholder management process.

What Is a Stakeholder?

A stakeholder is an individual or organization that is either actively involved in the project or who might be affected by the project's execution or completion. It is important to note that the stakeholders may be either positively or negatively affected by the project, so it is crucial to identify all of them—not just those who are positively affected. To expand on the definition above, I think it is important for the project manager to be aware that there are those who think they are stakeholders but who may not be in the strict sense of the word. Actually, those people can do the most damage to the project. If you ignore someone who thinks he is a stakeholder and he happens to wield a tremendous amount of influence in the organization, he can kill the project before you even know what happened. So here is my simple definition of a stakeholder: A stakeholder is anyone who thinks he has a vested interest in the project.

Stakeholders need to be identified as soon as possible. Usually, most of the stakeholders can be identified during the requirements definition stage. While the project manager has the initial team together, she should properly identify stakeholders, using the experiences of the team members.

Identifying Stakeholders

Many stakeholders are obvious. Stakeholders include:

- ✔ Project team members
- ✔ The customer
- ✔ Functional managers
- ✔ Suppliers
- ✔ System users

There are also stakeholders who are not so obvious, including:

- ✔ Stockholders
- ✔ Local and federal regulating agencies
- ✔ Creditors
- ✔ Environmental groups

Then there are those who also think they are stakeholders. A good rule of thumb to use when identifying stakeholders is that it is far better to overdo it than to ignore someone. Once the project is under way and the project manager has an opportunity to interface with each stakeholder, he can begin to assess who is a true stakeholder and who has the power to impact the project. In that regard, it is helpful to have a stakeholder analysis process in place.

Stakeholder Analysis

Stakeholder analysis involves answering four basic questions:

1. Who is the stakeholder (or potential stakeholder)?
2. What is the stakeholder's position, relative to supporting the project?
3. What is the reason for the stakeholder's position?
4. What is the strategy for changing the stakeholder's position if it is less than positive?

Exhibit 5-3 is a simple form that can be used to help determine how to manage your stakeholders.

The most important aspect of the stakeholder analysis, after

Stakeholders	Position			Reason for Position	Strengths & Weaknesses	Strategy for Changing Position
	+	0	−			

Exhibit 5-3. Stakeholder analysis form.

identifying the stakeholder, is determining her position or agenda. What the project manager needs to know early in the project's life is whether the stakeholder is for, against, or neutral about the project, and whether the stakeholder will actively support or resist the project. Then, of course, it is important to determine why the stakeholder has taken that position.

A stakeholder will support or resist a project for a variety of reasons. The most basic reason for supporting a project is because it appears to be one that supports the organization's strategic goals. The stakeholder may dislike a project because it does not appear to support the goals. In any case, the reasons for support or resistance have to be known, otherwise the project manager has no chance to meet or change stakeholder expectations.

Once you know why the stakeholder takes the position he has chosen, you need to determine the stakeholder's strengths and weaknesses. Some strength and weakness considerations are:

- ✔ Political alliances
- ✔ Availability and effective use of resources
- ✔ Quality of decisions and managerial strategies
- ✔ Organizational support
- ✔ Dedication of support

Determining the stakeholder strengths and weaknesses helps the project manager assess just how important a particular stakeholder is to the project, both in terms of being a friend who can help obtain resources, for example, and as an adversary who can make obtaining resources very difficult. It is also important to know whether the stakeholder has enough organizational clout to actually impact the project.

Finally, it is crucial to develop a strategy to change a stakeholder's position if it is neutral or negative. A neutral position can be tolerated, although it is certainly better if all stakeholders support the project unconditionally. The chances are that a neutral stakeholder really doesn't have a stake so strong that she will sabotage the project. But a stakeholder with a negative bias is another thing altogether. At the very minimum, that stakeholder will not support your efforts to complete the project and at the worst case, he will actively lobby to kill the project.

Stakeholder Management Strategies

The most effective stakeholder management strategies are those that satisfy the stakeholder's requirements and answer their concerns. There are a variety of strategies that achieve these ends.

Two underused strategies that I have seen hook stakeholders immediately in the early stages of the project are the project charter and the project kick-off meeting.

The project charter is an internal document prepared by the senior management in conjunction with the project manager that briefly outlines the project scope, names the project manager, identifies the required resources, and establishes the communication plan for the project. The charter is the primary vehicle for identifying the parameters of the project and can be a powerful communication and negotiation tool. But perhaps its most important use is for obtaining buy-in from all the functional managers because they all have to sign the charter indicating that they support the project. Exhibit 5-4 shows a general project charter outline. Some organizations have much more detailed charters—some may even attach scope statements and, in some cases, the project plan. But the primary purpose of the charter is to name the project manager, explain the boundaries of her authority and responsibility, and detail the functional groups' project support responsibilities.

The kick-off meeting is another excellent opportunity to engage stakeholders and get their buy-in. There are usually two meetings that come under this heading. The first is generally very informal and simply announces that the project is approved to start—an announcement of the project's existence. The second one is more formal and is designed to discuss the project's scope,

I.   Purpose
II. Project Establishment
III. Project Manager Designation and Authority
IV. Project Manager Responsibility
      a. Support organization's responsibilities
      b. Project organization and structure
      c. Project team composition
V.   Communication Plan
VI. Definitions
VII. Appendixes

Exhibit 5-4. Project charter outline.

as much of the technical approach that is known, any issues expected, schedules, and budget. The amount of information provided at this kick-off meeting is entirely dependent on how far planning has progressed. But the opportunity to include the stakeholders is obvious. For instance, they can be engaged in the discussion about the technical approach and any risks or issues that they might know.

There are several other strategies or opportunities for making stakeholders feel a part of the project. Some of the most common strategies for satisfying stakeholder requirements and answering their concerns are:

✔ Actively involving them in the project

✔ Providing regular progress reports

✔ Including them in formal briefings and project reviews

✔ Providing them with individual briefings (particularly if an individual has a particular concern)

✔ Soliciting their advice (whether it is actually needed)

✔ Including them in major project strategy decisions

✔ Providing them with project reports and progress summaries.

Sometimes your strategy will not work or it is simply the wrong strategy for a particular stakeholder. But every strategy plan should include an assessment of the stakeholders' likely reactions and have an alternative strategy ready to implement.

Stakeholder Reactions and Alternative Approaches

Stakeholder reactions generally are predictable, especially if the stakeholder is positive about the project or even neutral. But it is those who are negative about the project who usually require more than one strategic thrust before they are won over. So be prepared for a lukewarm or even cold reception to your first try at answering the concerns of these stakeholders. First of all, your perception of their concerns, even if the stakeholder has expressed them, may not reveal the real concerns. For example, a stakeholder may say he is not convinced the technical approach is viable when his real issue is that he was not included in developing the approach. Hidden agendas proliferate in the stakeholder world. Be prepared to offer a strategy, then observe the reaction and adjust the strategy. That's the essence of stakeholder management.

Implementing the Strategy

When you finally develop your strategy and are ready to implement it, there are several considerations that need to be addressed. Ensure that:

- ✔ Management understands the impact of both supportive and adversarial stakeholders to a project's success.
- ✔ Stakeholder assessment is solicited in review meetings as a part of determining project status.
- ✔ Communication with stakeholders is maintained to improve their perception of the project's progress.

   ✔ An explicit evaluation of probable stakeholder response to major project decisions is accomplished.

   ✔ An ongoing, up-to-date report of stakeholder status is provided to key managers, principally to the project sponsor.

   ✔ Security of sensitive project information is maintained.

One of the unpleasant and politically damaging aspects of stakeholder management for the project manager is the need to keep some senior management informed about the stakeholder status—for or against the project. The project manager needs to have a significant emotional intelligence level to make senior management aware of stakeholder status without seeming to be working behind its back for malevolent reasons. In short, your purpose is not to be a tattletale or a whiner but to maintain strong stakeholder support for the project. This situation is not so difficult if the project has a sponsor who can help with stakeholder management.

Evaluating the Results and Adjusting the Strategy

After the strategy is implemented, you can evaluate the stakeholder response by simply soliciting her comments and reactions to what you have presented. If the strategy involved some change to a project process of the technical approach or utilization of resources, say, then be prepared to discuss in detail the positive impact you expect to the project. To reassure the stakeholder, you should also plan an after-action meeting to report on the strategy's actual impact to the project.

Again, be prepared to discuss and defend your planned strategy for answering particular concerns and issues, but also be prepared to adjust the strategy if it is clear the stakeholder is not happy with your approach. Sometimes a simple compromise is all that is needed to get a consensus between you and the stakeholder. However, you also have to recognize when the stakeholder is pushing the strategy into one that can negatively impact the project. For example, radically changing the product design has implications for the schedule, the budget, and the scope. This type of situation can be smoothly handled with an experienced and well-prepared project manager, but in extreme cases it calls for additional help from the project sponsor or even other senior managers.

Summary

The traditional practice of hiring IT professionals on the basis of their intelligence quotient is rapidly being replaced by the notion of looking first at the emotional intelligence level of the individual. There have been several studies during the past decade that unequivocally show that those members having significantly high EQs outperform those who have high IQs but low to average emotional intelligence.

Staffing a project can be a challenge for the project manager because of competition for resources from other project initiatives within the organization. The project manager needs to have strong negotiation and communication skills to successfully compete for the resources he and his initial project team have identified for the project.

Finally, one of the most difficult but most important tasks the project manager faces is that of managing the stakeholders. Generally, there are eight steps or activities in the stakeholder management process.

1. Identify the stakeholders.
2. Gather information on the stakeholders.
3. Determine the stakeholders' positions relative to the project.

4. Determine the stakeholders' strengths and weaknesses.
5. Develop a stakeholder management strategy.
6. Predict stakeholder reaction and prepare alternative strategies.
7. Implement the stakeholder strategy.
8. Evaluate the results and adjust the strategy.

Notes

1. W.G. Bennis and B. Nannus, *Leaders: The Strategies for Taking Charge* (New York: Harper & Row, 1985).
2. James M. Kouzes and Barry Z. Posner, *The Leadership Challenge* (San Francisco: Jossey-Bass, 1989).
3. J. Davidson Frame, *Managing Projects in Organizations, Revised Edition* (San Francisco: Jossey-Bass, 1995).

Chapter 6

Developing the Information Technology Project Plan

Successful projects, those that have been completed on time and budget and have satisfied the customer's requirements, are the projects that are carefully and well planned. In fact, if you examine successful projects closely, you will notice that they have two things in common. First, a lot of time is spent on the planning and development process, sometimes longer than it takes to complete the rest of the project. Second, approximately half the project budget will be expended before the implementation phase starts. Putting so much effort into the planning phase, or stated another way, waiting so long to get into the doing activities, is simply anathema to our culture. We want to get in there and code like hell. Nevertheless, it is important to remember that the success of a project starts with the project plan.

The project plan, like any plan, is only as good as the thought and care given to its development. One thing that has to be understood from the beginning is that the plan is dynamic—planning must evolve with the project. The more common practice is to develop a plan, put it on the shelf, and never look at it again until the project is finished. To successfully complete an IT project, the initial project plan needs to be as thorough and detailed as possible. The trick is to update and change the plan as more is known about the project, the evolving technical approach, the risks, and the customer's view about what the final product will look like. In many IT projects, the requirements themselves are evolutionary. That is, the customer does not have a clearly defined image of the final product, only a sense of the general functionality that is needed. With an evolving requirements definition process, the plan must also be flexible and evolving. Even if the project is very well defined from the beginning, which is difficult to do in today's fast-paced business and technology environment, there needs to be a refreshed plan for, at the very minimum, every one of the project's phases.

This chapter discusses how to develop the project plan and provides a project plan outline that can be used, with only moderate alteration, for virtually any IT project.

Before writing the project plan, a significant amount of work is required. These first steps are crucial. The considerations included in the plan will spell the difference between project success and failure.

Planning Considerations

At the very minimum a project plan must answer these three questions:

1. What is to be done?
2. When should it be done?
3. Who should do it?

The project plan generally starts taking shape as soon as a project manager is assigned to the project. The project manager will have some idea of what is required from the scope statement, contract documents if it is an external project, or any information gleaned from those who selected the project or directed that it be done. If the project manager was fortunate enough to have been included in the embryonic stage of the project, then she is way ahead of the learning curve. Otherwise, she must resort to other means to determine what the project is all about.

Determining What to Do

We explored this subject in some detail in the last chapter, but it is beneficial to review the process.

Determining what to do is simple in concept, but not always easy to accomplish. The difficulty of determining project requirements is directly linked to how detailed and well written the customer's needs are stated. That seems simple enough, but the fact is, more than half of all projects start out with poorly stated or poorly conceived project requirements. So the project manager must first determine what is to be done. He must ask this question: Why are we doing this project?

If the SOW, contract documents, or other written documentation define the project requirements, then determining what is to be done is generally a matter of restating the requirements in a work breakdown structure format and assigning tasks and responsibilities. If the project is internal to the organization, or the customer is not sure what he wants, then the project manager has to determine the requirements. Determining the requirements under these circumstances is done by asking a lot of questions—questions of those who selected or generated the project and questions of those who are for and against the project. Remember that it is just as important, if not more so, to know who is against the project, and why, as it is to know who is for the project. This is because the relative strength of these stakeholders in the organization can shape the final requirements. Without knowing the individual stakeholders' agenda, the project manager quickly finds himself pursuing requirements that are being subtly changed by a powerful functional manager.

Determining when the project's deliverables are due drives the number of resources required and vice versa. My personal approach is to first determine when the customer needs the product and then to determine how many and what type of resource skills it will take to complete the job. What I discover from this exercise determines whether I need to acquire more resources, either internally or externally, or whether I need to renegotiate with the customer. In short, the schedule, numbers or resources, and budget are so interrelated that they generally have to be analyzed and developed together. But the first step is to determine when the project's deliverables are due.

Determining When It Should Be Done

The schedule is driven by first to market considerations, the customer's operational needs, or maintaining or creating market share. No matter the reason, the project manager's job is to determine how the schedule can be met.

Almost every project has a dictated schedule, and it is almost always an unreasonable one. Customers do not want to hear that the schedule is unreasonable; they want to know how you are going to meet it. If this sounds far-fetched or even crazy, you may be right on both counts. The reality is that schedules are set for, at least in the customers' minds, very good and plausible reasons, and it is the responsibility of the providing organization to meet schedules. Therein lies a major communications gap between the provider and the customer, and it is one that usually results in project failure or at least less than satisfactory project success. The sad reality is that there is little that can be done to correct the problem. So what is the project manager to do?

Determining the schedule is straightforward. First, the project documentation will very likely contain a "deliver by no later than" date, that is, a delivery milestone. If so, the schedule is fixed. The task then is to determine whether the date can be met. Usually, the schedule, even an unreasonable one, can be met given enough resources. The problem, of course, is that there may not be enough resources in the company, which requires hiring or contracting for additional skills. Even when there are enough resources, there is a break-even point beyond which it becomes cost-prohibitive.

If the customer does not dictate the schedule—an unusual occurrence, but it happens occasionally—then the project manager and her team can develop a schedule based upon the numbers and skill sets needed. Actually, this is a best-case scenario, and one that the project manager should lobby for because the resulting schedule is reasonable and likely to be met.

The usual scenario for determining the schedule is that the requirements are determined, a WBS is developed, and a network, usually a precedence diagram, is drawn to show the task dependencies. From the network analysis, a good estimate of the schedule can be determined. It is important to remember that when determining task durations for the network analysis, the number and skill sets available for the task have to be considered. Otherwise, the estimate will be inaccurate, and the schedule will not be achievable. Once the network is drawn and analyzed, it is a simple matter to determine the shortest duration for completing the project and whether it is possible to accomplish the project in the time allowed by the customer. If not, then the project manager and his organization can make the decision about how to shorten the schedule—usually this involves who is needed for the project, which is the next important planning consideration.

Determining Who Should Do It

During teaching or speaking opportunities, I often ask whether anyone belongs to an organization that assigns team members to the project as opposed to having the project manager determine who is needed and then negotiating for them. Usually there are a few people who have their resources assigned, so the practice is not uncommon. But more commonly, it is left to the project manager to analyze the need, determine the skill sets required, and then to negotiate for the resources.

Logically, one would expect determining the team makeup to be a relatively straightforward, if not simple, task. The project manager probably knows everyone in the organization and probably has worked with most, if not all, of them. With relatively small or not too complex projects and in smaller organizations, the task of determining skill sets and available resources is actually not too difficult. It is with complex projects, requiring widely different skill sets and cutting across several functional lines, that the task becomes enormous.

The best approach for determining required resources is to elicit the help of what I call an initial team. This team is composed of other experienced project or functional managers and other senior personnel. I call it an initial team because these people will not function as team members once the project gets under way—they are too senior to work as project team members. The function of this initial team is to help the project manager analyze and define the project requirements and to determine the skill sets needed. Once the skill sets are known, the resources can be identified, and this initial team will be able to recommend specific people to serve on the project team.

When negotiating for resources, it is very important to remember that one should ask for a specific person. If the functional manager from whom the resource is requested is not presented with the name of a specific individual, then she will likely provide the first available person, regardless of whether he has the requisite skills and experience. Asking specifically for someone may not yield the desired result, that is, the individual may not be available because he is committed to other projects, but it alerts the functional manager to the specific level of skill and experience needed for the project. From a negotiating perspective, this approach puts the onus on the manager to provide someone of equal or better qualifications.

After the resources are identified and their use on the project guaranteed, the project plan can be more fully developed.

The IT Project Plan

It is surprising how many organizations begin projects without having spent time planning for them. There is the code like hell syndrome, which is to begin coding before a plan is in place. This syndrome is based on the belief that all things can be fixed with software. Furthermore, those who practice this syndrome believe there is no time waste. Another often heard question is: Why spend the time planning when technology changes so rapidly anyway?

In a well-planned project, the cost of analyzing requirements, building a project team, planning the project work, designing and optimizing the deliverables, and hiring vendors or teammates can easily consume 50 percent of the project budget before the project is ever implemented. Without a plan, preparing and controlling this expenditure is not possible.

Project planning is necessary and important. If it is done correctly and the organization supports it, approximately 50 percent of the project's budget is used up by the time the project itself is implemented. That means that half the budget is spent on analyzing the requirements, building the project team, planning the work, and designing the deliverables. Without a plan, none of this is possible.

Plans vary from industry to industry and from organization to organization. However, all project plans have basic components. The next section describes a generic project plan that can be tailored to any industry.

The IT Project Plan Format

Exhibit 6-1 illustrates a generic project plan format. This format has been developed over many years by practicing project manager in various industries. The plan's components are discussed below so that you understand what is typically provided in each

I.   Executive Summary
II.   Project Description
       a. General description of the project
       b. Project objectives
       c. Project fit with strategic goals
III.   Technical Approach
IV.   Contractual Requirements
V.   Resource Requirements
       a. Equipment
       b. Materials
       c. People
VI.   Schedules
       a. Master schedule
       b. Detailed phase schedules
       c. Milestone chart
       d. Deliverable schedule
       e. Meetings or other customer-required schedules
VII.   Cost Estimates and Budget
VIII. Potential Risks
IX.   Evaluation Criteria
X.   Appendixes
       a. Systems engineering management plan
       b. Risk plan
       c. Communication plan
       d. Logistics or other special-purpose plans

Exhibit 6-1. A generic project plan format.

section and so that you can easily adapt the sections to your own
organization and project.

Executive Summary

The executive summary is written last because it is meant to be a
short description of the project and it is intended for senior man-

agers. The idea is to provide a description of the project that key stakeholders can quickly read and digest without burdening them with technical details—a synopsis of the reasons for the project and its major characteristics and functional capabilities. If a stakeholder needs more information, she can get it from the remainder of the project plan.

The executive summary should be viewed as exactly that—a summary. It usually is relatively short, about two pages, but can be longer, depending on the size and complexity of the project. It should be written as succinctly as possible so that readers can quickly read and digest it but still be able to talk about the project with some authority.

Project Description

This section provides a narrative description of how the project manager and team will accomplish the project's goals. It should describe both the management and the technical approaches to accomplishing the project. Precise details of how to manufacture a part or of the steps in developing some software are not required, but the general processes of each step of the project should be described.

This section should also discuss the relationship of the project's technical approach to existing technologies. If it is anticipated that new and different technologies will be required, this section should discuss how they would be integrated into the project.

This section also describes the requirements of the project, the objectives, the scope (how large the project is), the time line, the type and number of end products, what the measure of success will be, and how the project goals mesh with the organization's goals. This section is usually very detailed and can be several pages long.

Technical Approach

This section is an opportunity for the project manager and project team to explain what processes are required to achieve the goals of the project. Both the management and technical processes should be outlined here. It is not necessary to describe the exact manufacturing steps of building a piece of equipment, but the general processes of each step of the project should be described.

This section should also discuss the relationship of the project's technical approach to existing technologies. If it is anticipated that new and different technologies are required, then this section will discuss how these new technologies will be integrated into the project. Remember that rapidly changing technologies are a burden and one of the primary risks in attempting an IT project. Therefore, it is to the project manager's benefit to have a plan for dealing with these changes before they occur. Not only is it wise to be ready to cope with such changes, but your project stakeholders will certainly feel more comfortable with your leadership.

Contractual Requirements

Often this section will not apply to your project, but occasionally a project comes about because of an external contract. In this case, there are some specific and far-reaching contractual clauses that must be considered before the project progresses too far. For example, it is common in the public sector to let a contract for a needs analysis. In such cases, the buyer, in this case a government agency, always stipulates that the contractor performing the work will not be allowed to bid on any resulting follow-on contracts. This type of special contractual requirement needs to be in the project plan because all stakeholders need to be reminded, in writing, that this project will end the organization's participation in the work that follows.

Other contractual requirements that should be mentioned in this section include customer-mandated milestones or special reporting requirements—anything that the project manager feels should be brought to the attention of key stakeholders.

Resource Requirements

Resources include anything needed to accomplish the project's goals. The resource of greatest concern is people to work the project. That is because projects usually start with inadequate numbers of people or with individuals who possess less than acceptable skills. Some resources, such as materials or equipment, are easy to acquire—but acquiring the right people for the job is not so easy. Other major resource requirements include special equipment, such as computers, special test equipment, or desks and office space, and any kind of materials, that is, hardware, special connectors, or cabling.

It is important to break out these costs for several reasons. First, it is easier for the project manager to negotiate for resources if he can enumerate them precisely. Second, it really is the only way to identify the exact project costs. Third, having a detailed accounting of costs enables the project manager and team to determine where cost cuts can be made without jeopardizing the project.

Schedules

The schedule section of the project plan quickly becomes unwieldy. My personal preference is to give a brief overview of the schedule requirements, perhaps a milestone chart as well, and then attach the schedules as an appendix. This approach serves two purposes: First, it eliminates the necessity of having foldouts to accommodate the size that schedules generally require, and second, appendixes are easy to detach and use as a separate document. Initially, of course, the appendixes need to be a part of the plan for approval purposes and so that the whole plan approach is understandable. But considering that there can be a number of schedules (master, task, milestone, meetings, and so on), summarizing them in this section and attaching them as appendixes makes a lot of sense.

One thing that many new project managers don't understand, or are surprised by, is the number of meetings that a customer can require. For example, I once had a government customer who required that we schedule a meeting every two weeks for the duration of the project, which was three years long. The project plan contained only one schedule of meetings.

One other important type of scheduling tool that is often overlooked for this section is the network analysis. A network analysis, either a PERT or precedence diagramming analysis, is required to determine the critical path and other risk areas. The schedule section is the place to show this analysis.

Financials

The WBS is the key project management tool. With it, the project requirements are completely captured along with the tasks needed to accomplish the work of producing the deliverables. With the project tasks identified, the schedules are developed with a PERT or precedence diagram. So the WBS must be developed first, then the schedule.

After the schedule is set and the number of resources are determined, the cost estimates can be developed. Some project management specialists determine the schedule before resources are considered; others determine the available resources, then develop the schedules around them. The fact is, these two approaches to planning have to be worked together. That is, one cannot determine the schedule without having determined the resources. Likewise, the schedule, particularly if the customer sets it, can drive the number of resources required. Hence, schedule and resource analyses must be done together and the appropriate trade-offs made to optimize both factors.

Usually, the project is approved and ready to begin before the project manager is even assigned. The best-case scenario is one that includes the project manager in the analysis and selection of the project. If, however, the project manager suddenly finds himself in charge of a project with no knowledge of its beginnings, it is indeed wise to verify the budget. The project manager should always determine whether the assigned budget is adequate to accomplish the project requirements. After all, if the project is a success, perhaps the project manager will get the credit. But if it is a failure, the project manager certainly will be held responsible. Developing a cost estimate to verify adequacy of the budget may not get the budget changed, but it will allow the project manager to document that the analysis was accomplished and the key stakeholders were notified. At the very least, the project manager and team will know whether they have to cut costs to meet the given budget.

Potential Risks

Analyzing project requirements is the first opportunity to identify potential risks. It is imperative that any potential risks are identified and documented in this section. Furthermore, a contingency plan to handle these risks is crucial. Generally, the type of risks that surface this early in the project revolve around resources and, often, schedule. For instance, a requirement needing the services of specialized skills not resident in the organization poses a significant risk to the project's success. Also, if the customer sets the schedule because of, say, some operational or marketing need, then this might increase the risk to the success of the project. These risks should be identified in this section. In the previous examples, a plan that provides a contingency contract with a vendor or consultant who has the requisite expertise and the addition of resources to reduce the time it takes to accomplish the work should be provided, respectively. However, remember that adding resources generally does not result in reducing the schedule in the

IT industry. In fact, adding resources often increases the time to finish a task or project because of the learning curve required to bring new resources up to speed. (This is not the case in other engineering or construction projects—adding resources usually reduces the schedule significantly.)

Clearly, the project team will not be able to identify all the project risks, but with experience, the use of the initial team, the WBS, the network diagram, and general lessons learned information, many of the likely risks can be identified. One very good way of capturing these potential risks in this section is with a matrix similar to Exhibit 6-2. This matrix identifies the risk, its level (high, medium, or low), a brief description of how the risk will be dealt with, and the risk level after the contingency plan is implemented.

The matrix usually will contain ten to twelve risks, the approximate number that a team can actively monitor and control at any one time. The real importance of such a matrix is to communicate to the major stakeholders and especially to the customer. This matrix clearly identifies the risk, the risk level, the strategy for mitigating the risk, and how the strategy will reduce the risk level when it is implemented.

Risk identification begins with requirements definitions and continues throughout the project's life cycle. The primary tools that will help the project team identify risks are the WBS, because identifying tasks to meet the requirements will reveal resource, schedule, quality, and technology shortcomings in the organization, and the network diagramming techniques, because networks reveal interrelationships.

Once these key sections of the plan have been developed, it is time to consider how you will know whether the project is progressing satisfactorily. The section on evaluation criteria tells you what you need to do to find out.

Evaluation Criteria

The importance of establishing evaluation criteria designed to measure how well the project is doing against the customer's re-

RISK/CONTINGENCY PLAN ANALYSIS

Requirement	Risk	Risk Level	Contingency Strategy	Risk Level After Strategy Implementation
Deliver fully functional prototype within six months of contract date,	Customer is not clear on functional needs.	High	Involve customer in prototype design and development.	Low
Integrate new version of XYZ operating system into communications package.	No expertise with XYZ OS; don't know extent of defects in new version.	Medium	Hire XYZ developing company to integrate new OS version into the communications package.	Low
Provide 1,500 stations per month for customer operations.	Manufacturing capability currently at 1,300 per month.	High	Add second shift to manufacturing line.	Low to medium
Test first system by July 15.		Medium	Test software code as it is written.	Low

Exhibit 6-2. Risk analysis and contingency strategy matrix.

quirements cannot be overstated. The customer may mandate some evaluation criteria in the form of product demonstrations, status reviews, or tests. Furthermore, standards established by the industry, regulatory agencies, or environmental groups define processes or procedures for the organization. But the project manager and her team also have to establish criteria against which to measure whether they are meeting the project requirements. These criteria may include milestones, sign-off points by the customer, or quality checks by the project manager or, more appropriately, by an independent person or group. One good way of evaluating the project is to have an independent team perform a technical and financial audit on the project at various points in the schedule. Project teams do not generally view audits very favorably because the very word implies looking for something wrong and, more to the point, attaching blame for whatever is uncovered. But audits are important tools in the business of managing projects. If they are thoughtfully introduced and intelligently used, that is, not for punishment but for improvement, they become a very powerful means of evaluating the project's work.

One other major section of the IT project plan is often overlooked, or at the very least, shortchanged. This section deals with ancillary and additional plans or other informational documents that are pertinent to the project and/or important to the project team and stakeholders. This section is the appendixes.

Appendixes

The appendixes are a very good place to collect additional required plans and such things as schedules. I always attach my schedules and network analyses as an appendix because, first, they tend to be bulky and are usually on foldouts and, second, schedules and network diagrams are the kinds of things that the project manager and her team need to constantly consult. As appendixes, they are easily detached for daily use. More important, the appendixes are the place for other project-related plans, specifications, and engineering drawings.

Often, because of specialized needs, the customer will include specifications about the products needed. Let us say, for example, that the project is to develop and build a communication link to a remotely controlled drone for the military. In this case, the customer (the Department of Defense or the Central Intelligence Agency) would very likely include product specifications and perhaps even some engineering drawings of some of the components. If so, these documents would be attached to the project plan as appendixes.

Other appendix candidates are ancillary plans such as the risk plan, quality plan, the communication plan, and the systems engineering management plan. All these plans are important to the project team and have to be available for their use before the major work on the project begins. If the project has resulted from a contract outside the organization, particularly if the customer is from the federal sector, then these plans will have been required and will have to be approved by the customer. Even if the project is one internal to the organization, developing the plans before work on the project begins is crucial. This is because the project team usually doesn't have the time or the inclination to stop work and develop plans if they already are in the midst of completing their assigned project tasks.

The key to a successful project, or anything else for that matter, is a carefully thought-out plan. In the case of projects, it is absolutely imperative if the project has any hope of success. One problem all project managers have is getting the plan completed and in place before pressure from senior management requires that the project work, that is, actual designing, coding, and building, is begun. A phenomenon that plagues us all is the appearance that work is not being done unless we can actually *see* progress. Planning is a thinking and writing exercise and simply does not give the same appearance of movement that, say, writing code does. Thus, the project manager must find ways of convincing senior management that progress is being made even though the progress is largely mental. Whether the project requirements are met within the customer's expectations depends on how well the plan is developed and, of course, implemented.

Mapping the WBS to the Project Plan

In March 2001, the General Accounting Office (GAO) issued a report that discussed the importance of matching needs, that is, requirements, to resources, that is, supplier capability to perform. The report specifically looks at the Department of Defense and its general practice of contracting for large weapon systems, but the results of the GAO study are applicable to any project, public or private sector, large or small, complex or simple.[1] The findings, when viewed practically or logically, probably are not surprising. Yet, the very problem that the findings focus on is the problem that invariably dooms many IT, and other, projects. Namely, the customer's requirements are not matched to the existing resources *before* starting the product development cycle.

In the rush to start coding, euphemistically speaking, the project is started without giving proper consideration to the available resources—human, capital, or technical. In short, planning is rushed, incomplete, or not done at all. Consequently, the project is not successful in the sense of performing as one would hope or expect.

The GAO found that a match between a developer's resources and a customer's expectations is eventually met on just about every project's product. But the key distinction between successful products—those that perform as expected and are developed within estimated resources—and problematic products are *when* this match is achieved. When a customer's needs and a developer's resources were matched before a product development started, the more likely the development was to meet cost and schedule objectives. When this match took place later, after the product development was under way, problems occurred that took significantly higher investments—sometimes double—of time and money.

The study found three factors that were key to matching needs and resources before product development began. First, developers employed the technique of systems engineering to identify gaps between resources and customer needs before committing to a new product development. Second, customers and developers were flexible. Leeway existed to reduce or defer customer needs to future programs or to allow the developer to make an investment to increase knowledge about a technology or design feature before beginning product development. Third, the roles and responsibilities of the customer and the product developer were matched, with the product developer being able to determine or significantly influence product requirements. In cases where these factors were not present at program launch, product development began without a match between requirements and resources. Invariably, this imbalance favored meeting customer needs by adding resources, which resulted in increased costs and later deliverables.

Matching the customer's needs to the provider's resources would seem a logical thing to do. The fact is, though, many projects are begun with little thought and less planning. The only basis for the commitment in these cases is that the project seems doable and perhaps is similar to one that the organization has already done. Unfortunately for both the organization and the customer, even if the product is finally delivered with the functionality desired by the customer, it usually costs more and takes longer if the needs were not matched with the available resources before the product development began.

Validating the Schedule and Budget Estimates

Schedules and budgets are estimated for individual projects using the tools we discussed earlier—the WBS, network analysis, and

Gantt charts. But once these schedules and budgets are completed for each individual project, they have to be evaluated and validated in the context of the company's total program and portfolio activities, that is, each project is evaluated against all other projects across the company. Otherwise, there will be no sense of whether the company can manage all the projects with available resources or if the schedules can be met within the construct of resources allocated across multiple projects.

There should be at least two formal reviews for both the project's technical and cost approaches. The first review for the technical proposal (often called the blue team review) occurs fairly early in the process. The basic function of this review is to determine whether the customer's requirements are understood and the technical approach is viable. The second review, called the red team review, occurs near the end of the planning cycle and is a very thorough review of the proposed approach from the customer's perspective. This review addresses the customer's requirements, the technical approach, and, in short, whether all the requirements have been addressed. This review has to be accomplished late enough in the cycle that all the key elements of the plan are complete, but early enough to incorporate needed changes.

The first review for the cost detail is called the gold team review. This team looks at the approach, whether the costing team has considered all the customer requirements, and if the cost strategies are viable. The second review, the green team review, occurs approximately a week after the red team reviews the technical proposal. This timing is necessary in order to revise the costs if the red team uncovers omissions or other discrepancies in the technical approach.

Even when the costs have been reviewed and the green team agrees that the costs are comprehensive and accurate, the senior official responsible for the final cost document—or proposal, as the case may be—will want to review the costs, or at least the bottom line. The project manager and the costing person should be prepared to defend the cost figures and their rationale for them. The project manager should also be prepared to make a recommendation relative to how much profit to apply. Since profit is the only rate that is flexible, a smaller profit or even no profit can be used to reduce the overall price if the effort is a competitive bid, for example. The decision about how much or how little profit to use resides with the company president or a designated representative. However, the project manager should have an estimate of what the customer is willing to pay and what it will take to win the job. Thus, the amount of profit that keeps the price below the target price is the appropriate profit rate to apply to obtain the work. Exhibit 6-3 describes the schedule, cost, and resource estimating process.

Schedules and costs are intricately interwoven. They impact each other as one and then the other changes over time. But just as schedules and costs are intricately balanced, so are they both dependent upon how resources are allocated across the company's many projects.

Resource Allocations Across Multiple Projects

Addressing the skills and processes necessary to schedule shared resources across multiple projects (portfolio or program) requires an intimate understanding of all the resource skill and experience sets along with the tools to allocate and track these resources. Most standard project management software programs contain resource allocation modules, which not only track individual resources but how they are allocated, how much is allocated, and whether they are overallocated. These programs also produce reports that are the usual communication tools for stakeholder management. So learning how to use these tools is critical to successful project management, particularly in the program and portfolio environment. With these tools and the skills to use them we can:

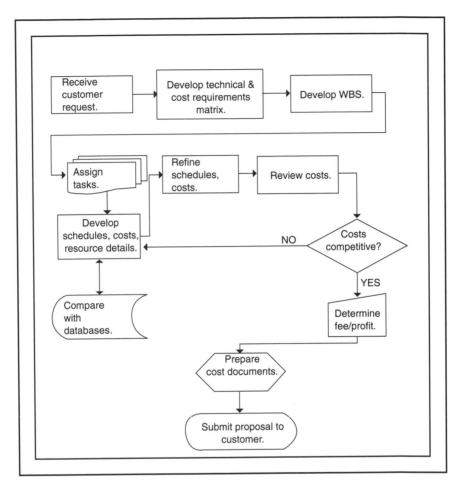

Exhibit 6-3. Sample schedule and cost-estimating process.

- ✔ Balance individual resource load versus capacity across the portfolio.
- ✔ Assign and allocate resource skills effectively across the portfolio.
- ✔ Understand shared resource availability.
- ✔ Make fact-based portfolio schedule trade-offs.
- ✔ Preserve project schedule priorities relative to enterprise objectives.

✔ Present useful status (high-level portfolio and detailed project) to stakeholders.

The resource allocation, in conjunction with the final schedule and cost evaluation and validation, is the last step before project plan approval and implementation.

Reviewing, Finalizing, and Implementing the Plan

Plans, by their very nature, are dynamic. The process of developing the project plan is dynamic if not sometimes chaotic, as can be seen from the many interleaving elements that force a balancing act. But once the plan is finalized, a review process should be developed and strictly adhered to. This is the time to get all stakeholders on board with the project and your approach to accomplishing it. Note that a plan is never final, nor is it ever completely accurate, at least at the stage before the project is implemented. This is because risk events occur, customers change the project scope, some task was overlooked, technology becomes obsolete, and the technical approach may not work as planned. Some or all of these things happen in every project, and that is why a project plan requires continuous updating.

The review process can be done with individual stakeholders, which can be time-consuming. Or it can be effectively done as a briefing or a series of briefings to the collective body of stakeholders. Usually, the latter is preferable because not only is it more efficient, but it provides a forum for discussion, which usually results in uncovering other concerns and issues that need to be addressed. In the end, all the stakeholders internal to the organization have to be convinced that the project is one that they can support and that supports the strategic goals of the organization. Once the internal stakeholders sign off on the plan, the customer then should also sign off. Usually, no one literally signs the project plan, but there is agreement, and official, written notification is provided to the organization (from the external customer) and the project manager. This is the final step before the project actually is implemented.

Project implementation is the actual start of project work. Although a lot of data gathering and even some high-level design work is a part of the plan development, the start of deliverable production can only begin when the plan is approved. Project implementation is usually officially acknowledged with a kick-off meeting, and the customer is invited to attend. After all, this is when we find out if the planning cycle was successful.

Summary

Project plans are dynamic—they have to evolve with the project because of the changing nature of projects. The most successful plans address these three elements:

1. What is to be done?
2. When should it be done?
3. Who should do it?

Answering these three questions determines the shape of the project, what its technical approach is going to be, what resource skill sets are needed and how many, how long it is going to take, and how much it is going to cost.

One key component to developing a successful plan is the review process. Often organizations do not provide formal reviews of the plan on the erroneous notion that there is not enough time in the planning cycle to accomplish them. But every minute spent in the planning cycle pays dividends in the long run. When things go wrong in the implementation phase, the company will rue its decision not to spend the extra week to thoroughly review the plan and to obtain buy-in from all the stakeholders.

Note

1. "Best Practices: Better Matching of Needs and Resources Will Lead to Better Weapon System Outcomes," General Accounting Office Report GAO-01-288 (March 2001).

Chapter 7

Risk Management in Information Technology Projects

The Nature of Risk

The life of a project manager is a life of conflict. In truth, project management is conflict management. The project manager's job is to smoothly negotiate the obstacles encountered during every phase of the project's life. If there was no risk or conflict in a project, there would be no need for a project manager—project management would become an administrative task. But risk is two-sided; there is the possibility of loss and the potential for gain. The risks in IT projects generally exhibit significant extremes of both sides—the losses are great if the risk event occurs unabated, but the gains can be immense if the risk is planned for and eliminated, or at least mitigated and made manageable.

This chapter discusses the basic definitions of risk and risk management. A risk management model and process are presented that will prepare the organization to plan for and reduce IT risks.

Risk Defined

Risk is characterized by three components:

1. The event (i.e., what can happen to the project, good or bad?)
2. The probability of event occurrence (i.e., what are the chances the event will happen?)
3. The impact to the project (i.e., what is the effect on the project, good or bad, if the event actually does occur?)

Types of Risk

There are two types of risks—business and pure, or insurable, risk. Risk is not necessarily negative; it may be an opportunity for gain. The key to risk management is recognizing the potential risk events and whether they can be directed and controlled for a neutral or positive effect on the project. If the risk event can only lead to negative impacts, then it should not be attempted; it should be avoided, transferred to someone else, or transferred to another organization.

Business Risks

A business risk is one that provides an opportunity for gain as well as for loss. An example of a business risk is a customer change to the project scope. The change might represent a risk to the provider because it involves skills or expertise the company does not possess. However, the scope change might produce additional revenue if the company can hire additional resources, team with another company, or hire a vendor to provide the necessary expertise. Business risks are the risks that can be managed. Management of insurable, or pure, risks should never be attempted.

Insurable or Pure Risks

Insurable risks, sometimes called pure risks because they offer only opportunities for loss, are risks that the organization should never take on. Incredibly, IT organizations routinely attempt such projects because of the prevailing view that everything can be fixed with software.

Some examples of insurable risks are natural disasters such as fires, floods, hurricanes, and earthquakes. For instance, if a company is located in a high-risk area for hurricanes, it will insure against such loss. But there are other, more subtle types of pure risk. Often a company will attempt a project because the major project requirements are within the company's capability, even though one or two other requirements may not be. Since they are qualified to accomplish the majority of a project's requirements, many companies make the assumption that they will be able to complete the rest. Mature, or learning, organizations recognize these disastrous situations and plan for them. These organizations have effective project selection and risk management processes. The project selection process was discussed in Chapter 3.

The risk management process is best understood through the use of a risk management model, such as the one discussed below. This risk management model can be applied in any organization and used in any industry.

A Risk Management Model

Risk management, like every critical management activity, is best accomplished when a formalized and documented set of guidelines and standard operating procedures are implemented and followed by everyone in the company. The Project Management Institute (PMI) has provided guidelines for a risk management process in their *Guide to the Project Management Body of Knowledge* (PMBOK Guide), including their own model. The model in

Exhibit 7-1 contains all the PMI model steps but is more detailed to better explain the risk management components and process elements. One key component of PMI's model that is implicit, but not stated, is that of continual evaluation. Risk management is an ongoing process that continues throughout the project's life cycle.

Planning Risk Management—The First Step

Risk planning should begin during the project selection phase. Project selection is the process of determining whether the company or organization should pursue a project. One criterion in the

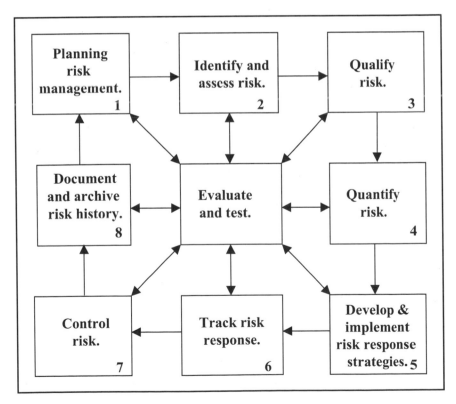

Exhibit 7-1. A risk management model.

selection process is risk—risk in the schedule, budget, resources available, expertise required, and fit with the organization's strategic plan.

The major inputs to the risk planning step are:

- ✔ The project charter
- ✔ Organizational policies or guidelines
- ✔ Contract documents (if the project results from an external customer; statement of work or other departmental project document if it is for an internal customer).
- ✔ The work breakdown structure (WBS)
- ✔ Network analysis

The project charter describes the project manager's limits of authority, the project priority, and the support requirements from various functional units in the organization. The project charter readily identifies many potential risk areas. For instance, if the project priority is four, then it is immediately apparent that the project can lose out if resources are tight. Other risks are not always so obvious. In fact, some risks may be so subtle that, if a project fails, they are never recognized. Consider, for example, this typical scenario in the IT environment: A project has the potential for propelling the organization into the next level of market competitiveness, if it is successful. Under this scenario, this type of project gets a great deal of senior-level scrutiny and guidance. It gets so much guidance, in fact, that senior management's good intentions hamper the project manager's efforts to the point of project failure. In other words, too much of even a good thing can interject risk into the project. Only a good project sponsor, charter, and mature senior management can prevent this kind of risk from occurring.

Along with the project charter, there are other company policies and guidelines to aid the project team. These policies and guidelines include templates, checklists, and guidance for identifying and planning risk contingencies.

Contractual documents, particularly those from external customers, contain information that can usually identify potential risk areas. This information has to be factored into the project planning. For instance, most contracts contain, at least, a high-level schedule. If a customer has a hard schedule completion date requirement, it may represent a potential risk to the seller, if resources are insufficient to meet the date.

The WBS is the most important tool for risk planning because it contains all the project tasks, and, consequently, a quick view of the potential risks. Since tasks drive the skill set and resource requirements, it will be apparent whether the project requires effort that falls outside the organization's capability—a critical risk that requires an alternative approach or a strategy to include teaming or outsourcing the work.

The network analysis provides insight into task interrelationships and potential risks associated with timing requirements and path convergence problems. Path convergence is the convergence of two or more network paths into a single node, as shown in Exhibit 7-2. In the exhibit, the convergence of paths from Tasks A, B, and C into Task D create greater uncertainties in starting

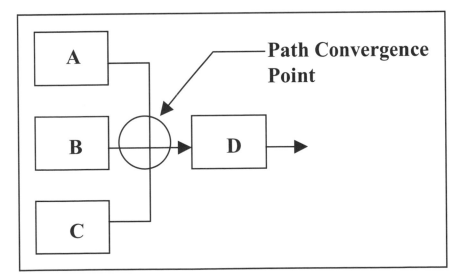

Exhibit 7-2. Path convergence in a network analysis.

the path out of D on time. If either of the durations for A, B, or C are in error, then the start time for D is affected. If all three are in error, then the start time of D is affected exponentially.

The major output of the risk-planning step is the risk management plan. The risk plan is a part of the overall project management plan and is often provided as an attachment. Many customers, particularly public sector customers, require a risk management plan as a part of any proposal submitted on a competitive bid. Exhibit 7-3 is an outline of a sample risk management plan.

Sections of the Risk Management Plan

The risk management plan guides you in the process of managing the risks of a particular project. Therefore, it is imperative that a plan is developed for every project and that the plan clearly identifies how the project risks will be identified, responded to, tracked,

---

Risk Management Plan

I. Project Name and Brief Scope Description
II. Risk Management Methodology
III. Roles and Responsibilities
IV. Funding
V. Risk Measurement and Interpretation Methodology
VI. Levels of Risk Response Responsibility
VII. Risk Communication Plan
VIII. Risk Tracking and Documentation
IX. Appendixes
    i. Risk table
    ii. Risk response plan

Exhibit 7-3. Risk management plan format.

and controlled. Let us look at the nine sections of the risk management plan.

1. ***Project Name and Brief Scope Description.*** This section provides the name of the project (and often the project manager's name) as well as a short description of the project's purpose.

2. ***Risk Management Methodology.*** This section provides a narrative about the tools or techniques used to identify the risks and how the risk response strategies will be determined. This section also contains the data sources from which the risk and risk strategies are developed, such as historical data from previous, similar projects.

3. ***Roles and Responsibilities.*** The roles and responsibilities of each project team member and other task contributors should be clearly defined in this section. If the responsibility to report, eliminate, or track a risk is not clearly assigned, a diligent team member can easily ignore an impending risk event. Of course, the project manager has ultimate responsibility for administering the risk plan and risk response strategies, but she can, and should, delegate responsibility for identifying risks and reporting triggers that presage a risk event.

4. ***Funding.*** Budgets for risk contingencies should be defined and guidance for their administration published at the start of the project. Many organizations assign the responsibility for the contingency, or reserve funding, pool to the project manager. However, funding for contingencies is strictly the responsibility of senior management in other organizations. This section of the risk management plan should clearly state how the contingency funding is to be administered.

5. ***Risk Measurement and Interpretation Methodology.*** The method or methods used to measure risk and interpret scores are defined in this section. Most companies have guidelines for applying a weighting factor and/or a score for each type of risk. Scoring methods are important in both the quantitative and qualitative analyses to reduce the effects of subjectively assigning a value

to a risk. Scoring methods should be chosen in advance, and they should be applied consistently throughout all steps of the risk management process.

6. *Levels of Risk Response Responsibility.* This section defines who has responsibility for each risk response according to a predetermined threshold. That is, during a project life cycle, risk events of different levels of impact can occur. The project manager has discretionary authority to handle certain levels of risk, but he must elevate the decision to a higher senior management position or to a committee, if the impact of the risk exceeds a certain monetary level. In some instances, only the customer has the authority to implement certain risk response strategies because of the costs to the project in time and money. The effectiveness of a risk management plan is measured against how well any actual risk event is kept below the lowest risk threshold.

7. *Risk Communication Plan.* This section describes report formats and outlines who receives reports on risk events, responses implemented, and the effectiveness of the risk response strategies.

8. *Risk Tracking and Documentation.* This section describes the process for tracking the effectiveness of the risk response strategies and how they are documented and archived as lessons learned.

9. *Appendixes.* This section provides a vehicle for attaching any additional information or plans, depending on the needs of each individual project. The two most common appendixes are the risk table and the risk response plan.

✔ *The Risk Table.* This is a table or matrix of all the identified risks in the project. Many project teams prefer that the table contains only those risks being managed at the moment and that it be revised as you deal with each risk.

✔ *The Risk Response Plan.* This is a detailed plan explaining the response strategies for each of the identified risks in the risk table.

Identifying and Assessing Risks—
The Second Step

Identifying risks is not a task that many project teams or organizations have done well in the past. Even today, risk identification and assessment, or the lack of it, is one of the key reasons that projects fail. In general, risk identification and risk management are not done well because of the difficulty in identifying risks. Given that risk is an uncertain and sometimes an unknown event, risk management tends to be viewed as more esoteric compared to the hard engineering components of the project. Therefore, many project teams and organizations are not as comfortable with it. Once a procedure for identifying risks is in place, however, managing them becomes less scary and much easier.

Risk identification is best accomplished with a team simply because the collective knowledge and experience of a group of people is far greater than an individual's can be. There are several methods useful in the process, but the best methods all are some variation of brainstorming. The brainstorming technique itself is generally the one method that yields the greatest number of identified risks because it is designed to produce a large amount of data in a relatively short period of time. Another technique especially useful for identifying sources of risk is the Ishikawa, or cause-and-effect, diagram. This diagram is also called the fishbone diagram because of its resemblance to the skeleton of a fish when it is completed. This technique is most often associated with quality analysis but can be used any time the objective is to identify the root causes of a problem. It has the added advantage of being a brainstorming technique as well and lends itself nicely to team development. Exhibit 7-4 is an example of how a cause-and-effect diagram can be used to identify software problem risks.

Checklists and Assumption Analysis

Historical data from the lessons-learned archives provides a rich source of information from which checklists can be developed.

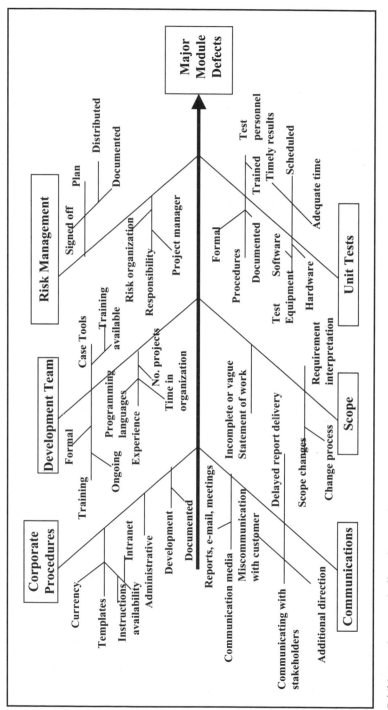

Exhibit 7-4. Cause-and-effect diagram for analyzing risk.

The organization's guidelines should include such a checklist. However, a word of caution: If they are used exclusively, checklists can create a false sense of security. The problem with checklists is that it is easy to assume every potentiality has been considered, if all the blocks are checked on the list. A checklist is simply a guide that contains the most common risks. Hence, it is only as good as the data used to develop it. The checklist is helpful and will reveal a number of potential risks, but the prudent project manager will use the checklist as one of several techniques for identifying her project risks.

All projects and project solutions are based on assumptions. Even the customer's scope statement is based on some assumptions. A major part of the risk identification process is an assumption analysis to determine assumption validity and whether any potential risks are present because of inaccurate, inconsistent, or incomplete assumptions.

An assumption analysis is best accomplished by listing all assumptions from scope statements, contract documents, and any other project descriptions in a matrix that describes each assumption and its rationale. Each of the assumptions can be checked against its reason and revised or discarded, depending on the validity of the rationale.

At this stage of risk planning, it is important that no filtering or prioritizing is attempted. The objective is to identify all potential risks. Filtering and prioritizing are techniques employed in the next step—qualifying the risks.

Qualifying Risks—The Third Step

Qualifying risks involves three components or substeps—filtering the risk to determine if it actually is a risk and when it is likely to occur during the project life cycle, determining the probability that a risk event will occur, and prioritizing the risk.

Risk Filtering

Once a list is developed, each risk is filtered to determine whether it is within project scope, if it is likely to occur, what its significance is, when it might occur within the project life cycle, and even if it is a real risk. It is not uncommon to identify a potential risk only to decide after careful deliberation that it is not a risk at all, or, if it is a risk, that the consequences of the impact are so small as to not be a concern. The best method for assessing risks is through a process of filtering, as the one shown in Exhibit 7-5. It is important not to prioritize risks at this stage. At this point of the analysis, the objective is to determine risk characteristics.

Many times a perceived risk is often not a risk when measured against the project scope. If the action generating the perceived risk is not within the scope, then it is not a risk and can be ignored.

Filtering the list developed during risk identification results in a final or revised risk list. The next step is to determine the probability of risk event occurrence. Whenever possible, it is better to assign a percentage probability to the risk. This is because the next step of the risk analysis process is to quantify the risk or measure the relative importance of one risk over another.

It is not always possible to assign a percentage probability when you lack historical data or experience. In those cases, the best that can be done is to assign a low, medium, or high probability of risk. Even in that case, a range of numerical values may be possible, as shown in Exhibit 7-6. Even taking the middle of the range, or being pessimistic and taking the high end of the range, provides a numerical result for a better comparison. The importance of assigning a percentage probability to the risk will become clear in the discussion on quantifying risks.

Prioritizing Risk

The risk-filtering step should result in a revised list of risks that accurately represent the most likely risk events to expect during a

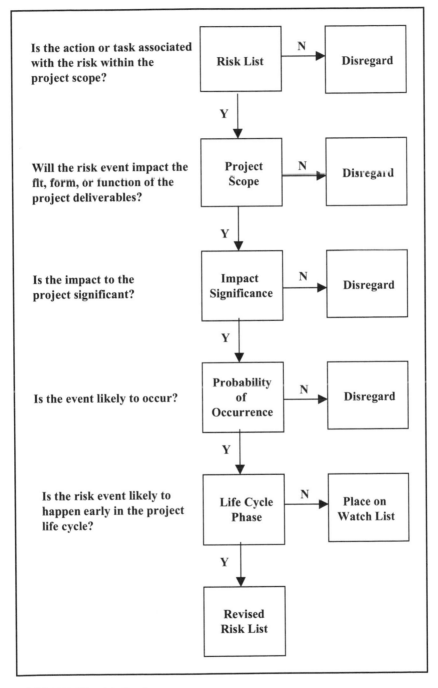

Exhibit 7-5. The risk-filtering process.

Risks	Very Low 0–5%	Low 6–15%	Medium 16–40%	High 41–80%	Very High 81–100%

Exhibit 7-6. Changing subjective ratings into percentages.

project's life cycle. Although it is important to identify potential risks, it is absolutely crucial to prioritize them. One serious mistake project managers make is to attempt to manage all risks on the revised list. Fortunately, that is not necessary because the reality is that we can manage about ten risks at a time. Hence, for greater efficiency and effectiveness, a list of the top ten risks should be actively managed with a watch list of the remainder to replace those that are mitigated, controlled, or eliminated, or that don't materialize. One of the best and easiest ways of prioritizing risks is with some form of a comparative ranking method. Exhibit 7-7 illustrates one such method.

Comparative ranking methods simply compare each risk against every other risk to determine its relative importance. Ranking is usually determined through voting and is best done as a team effort. The form in Exhibit 7-7 also provides for the application of a weighting factor to each of the risks. Organizations are either risk-prone, that is, willing to take more risks, or risk-adverse, unwilling to take much risk. The team will, therefore, assign a weighting factor to each type of risk to take into account the corporate risk-taking culture.

RISKS	Risk A	Risk B	Risk C	Risk D	Risk E	Risk F	Totals	Weight	T x W	Rank
Risk A										
Risk B										
Risk C										
Risk D										
Risk E										
Risk F										

Exhibit 7-7. Comparative risk-ranking form.

To use the comparative risk ranking form, the risks, A through F in our example, are listed down the left-hand side and across the top of the form. Then each risk is compared against every other risk in turn. If Risk A is considered more important, in terms of impact to the project, than Risk B, then in the square at the intersection of Risks A and B, write A = 1, as shown in Exhibit 7-8. Continue the process until every risk has been compared against every other risk. Total the scores for each risk (as

RISKS	Risk A	Risk B	Risk C	Risk D	Risk E	Risk F	Totals	Weight	T x W	Rank
Risk A							A=4			
Risk B	A=1						B=2			
Risk C	A=1	B=1					C=1			
Risk D	D=1	B=1	D=1				D=3			
Risk E	A=1	E=1	E=1	D=1			E=3			
Risk F	A=1	F=1	C=1	F=1	E=1		F=2			

Exhibit 7-8. Risk comparisons.

shown in Exhibit 7-9) and apply any weighting factors. The final ranking is shown in the last column. If each risk is considered to be of equal weight, then the scores will determine the relative ranking.

Quantifying Risks—The Fourth Step

Assigning a percentage value for risk probability creates opportunities for risk comparisons that wouldn't otherwise exist. The most difficult task throughout a risk analysis is estimating the probability of occurrence of the event with any degree of accuracy. One can argue that assigning a percentage of probability is very subjective and, therefore, inaccurate. However, it must be remembered that risks do not have to be measured in absolute terms to be of value; they can be measured relative to each other.

The most commonly used tool for determining the relative value of project risks is expected value. Expected value (EV) is a technique useful in assessing different technical approaches or making trade-off analyses. The concept is based on the probability of different outcomes occurring and explicitly considers the risk

RISKS	Risk A	Risk B	Risk C	Risk D	Risk E	Risk F	Totals	Weight	T x W	Rank
Risk A							A=4	.2	.8	1
Risk B	A=1						B=2	.2	.4	3
Risk C	A=1	B=1					C=1	.2	.3	4
Risk D	D=1	B=1	D=1				D=3	.2	.6	2
Risk E	A=1	E=1	E=1	D=1			E=3	.1	.3	4
Risk F	A=1	F=1	C=1	F=1	E=1		F=2	.1	.2	5

Exhibit 7-9. Weighted risk comparisons.

of the different approaches. That is, if there is a chance that one of several outcomes for a given scenario can occur, depending on the risks involved for each of the different conditions, then the most likely outcome over time can be determined. This most likely result is known as the expected value.

Expected value is based on the notion that each result is mutually exclusive. That is, the outcome is a random occurrence. A probability can be assigned to that outcome. Mathematically, expected value can be defined in this fashion. Suppose a random variable X, defined if the set of its possible values is given and if the probability of each value's appearance is also given, possesses n values. Then, these possible values (p) can be represented as X_1, $X_2, \ldots X_n$.

If $p_1, p_2, \ldots p_n$ are the probabilities associated with each X, then the *expected value* of X can be represented by the equation:

$$EV = \sum_{i=0}^{n} p_i X_i$$

The interpretation of this equation is that the expected value of an event is the sum of all the possible values of the variable multiplied by the probability of each of those values occurring. Expected value is generally used in conjunction with decision tree analyses, but can be used alone. The key point about expected value is that it is most effective when it is used to compare two or more potential outcomes, which helps eliminate some of the subjectivity in a risk analysis. An example will demonstrate how expected value is used.

Example

Your company runs a bus service in a midsize city. Currently, the company is using two bus models, both of which have exhibited frame defects over the past five years. The frame repairs cost an average of $500 per failure, but there has been only one failure per bus during a given year. The following table summarizes the data that have been collected on the frame failures.

Year	Model A (250 buses) Frame Repairs	Model B (175 buses) Frame Repairs
1	10	8
2	21	12
3	34	16
4	54	25
5	63	45

The company is considering replacing the current fleet with 500 new buses using either Model A or B. If Model A's original cost was $61,000 and Model B's cost was $64,000, with salvage values of $8,000 and $12,000, respectively, what would be the expected cost of each model? Assume that routine yearly repair costs for each model are the same. Using the five-year study data, decide which bus model is the best for the company based on expected cost as the decision criterion. Assume a 10 percent rate of return to calculate the net present value.

Solution

The first step in determining the expected cost for each bus is to figure the probability of failure occurrence. In this case, probability can be calculated for each year by dividing the number of failures per year by the total number of failures in each model. For example, in year one, Model A had ten frame failures requiring repair. The probability of a recurrence in year one for the new fleet of Model A buses will be 10/250 = .04, or 4 percent (number of failures divided by fleet size). For Model B, it will be 8/175 = .05, or 5 percent. The table below provides the probability of occurrence for each year and each model.

	Model A		Model B	
Year	Failures	Probability	Failures	Probability
1	10	0.04	8	0.05
2	21	0.08	12	0.07
3	34	0.14	16	0.09
4	54	0.22	25	0.14
5	63	0.25	34	0.19

The expected value of the repairs during year one for the new fleet of 500 buses can now be calculated by multiplying the probability of occurrence by the number of buses and by the average cost of each repair. Hence, for Model A, year one:

$$EV = .04 \times 500 \times \$500 = \$10,000$$

The following table summarizes the expected value for each year and each model.

	Model A	Model B
Year	Expected Value (probability × cost × no. buses)	Expected Value (probability × cost × no. buses)
1	10,000.00	12,500.00
2	20,000.00	17,500.00
3	35,000.00	22,500.00
4	55,000.00	35,000.00
5	62,500.00	47,500.00

Now determining the original cost and salvage value, we can construct an incremental table so that we can determine which of the two bus models represents the best value to the company. The original cost for Model A is $61,000, and for Model B it is

$64,000. The salvage value for Model A is $8,000 per bus, and for Model B it is $12,000 per bus. So for 500 buses:

	Model A	Model B
Original Cost	30,500,000.00	32,000,000.00
Salvage Value	4,000,000.00	6,000,000.00

The differential costs and benefits between the two models are:

	Year	Model A	Model B	Increment (B − A)
Original Cost	0	− 30,500,000	− 32,000,000	− 1,500,000
	1	− 10,000	− 12,500	− 2,500
	2	− 20,000	− 17,500	2,500
	3	− 35,000	− 22,500	12,500
	4	− 55,000	− 35,000	20,000
	5	− 62,500	− 47,500	15,000
Salvage Value	5	+ 4,000,000	+ 6,000,000	2,000,000

Calculating the net present value (NPV) will complete this analysis. But we must discuss present value (PV) first.

Present value is a financial calculation that takes into account the time value of money. That is, it is a way to estimate the future value of an investment or benefit as it is discounted over time. Mathematically, present value is determined by:

$$PV = \sum FV/(1 + i)^t$$

Where:

PV = present value of money

FV = future value of money

i = interest rate (often this is the internal rate of return or the cost of capital)

t = time period

n = number of time periods

$\sum$ = sum of PV of all the investments or benefits

NPV is defined as the difference between the present value of the benefits and the present value of the investments or costs. Mathematically, NPV is:

$$NPV = PV_{(Benefits)} - PV_{(Investments)}$$

A positive NPV is considered good since the benefits outweigh the investments; a negative result indicates that the venture (or project) is not a good investment.

Using the incremental differences in the analysis of the two buses, the NPV can be found by:

NPV = $-1,500,000/(1 + .10)^0 - 2,500/(1 + .10)^1 + 2,500/(1 + .10)^2 + 12,500/(1 + .10)^3 + 20,000/(1 + .10)^4 + 15,000/(1 + .10)^5 + 2,000,000/(1 + .10)^5$

and NPV = $-1,500,000 - 2272.73 + 2,066.12 + 9,391.44 + 13,660.27 + 9,313.82 + 1,241.84$

or   NPV = $-1,466,599.24$

Since the NPV is negative and the increment table was developed so that Model A is subtracted from Model B, that means that Model A has the largest benefit. Hence, the analysis indicates that Model A will be the most cost-effective choice of the two buses.

Notice that had NPV not been used to take into account the time value of money, that is, if a straight comparison between the costs and benefits of the two buses were done, then it would erroneously appear that Model B is the best value.

Decision Trees

A decision tree is a graphical way of representing the various possibilities or choices available in a decision-making process. The key to success in using decision trees is to identify all the possible outcomes. Decision trees also use probabilities in determining the likelihood of one outcome over another, so it is important to have as good a history of event results as possible. Finally, expected value is used to determine the most likely value of a particular branch in the decision tree. Although probabilities will be subjective to a large degree, the use of expected value with decision trees does provide a relative comparison of possible outcomes so that better-informed decisions can be made. Exhibit 7-10 is an example of how the decision tree is developed and used for decision making.

The square boxes in the decision tree represent decision points from which various decision paths can be taken. The circles, or nodes, represent points at which various outcomes might occur. In the example, the first decision to be made is whether to even develop the particular product. Not to develop the product could save the company $2 million, which might be the choice if there were other more technically and financially promising products being considered. Assuming the decision was made to pursue

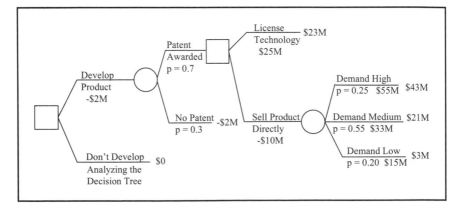

Exhibit 7-10. Research and development decision tree.

the product for the estimated development cost of $2 million, the next decision is dependent upon whether the company can obtain a patent for the product. The probability of obtaining the patent is 70 percent, but there is likewise a 30 percent chance the patent won't be awarded. Without the patent, the project might not be strategically viable and will be stopped. One benefit of the decision tree analysis process is that it provides go/no-go decision points that allow the company to end the project when it is obvious that continuing it would not meet long-term strategic goals.

The figures on the "High, Medium, and Low" branches from the "Sell Product Directly" node are estimates of what the revenues might reasonably be, based on market and competitive analyses. Thus, it is expected that there will be a 25 percent probability that the revenues will be $55 million. The $43 million figure at the end of the branch represents the net revenues that are expected if the "Demand High" branch actually materializes. In other words, when we subtract the $10 million costs for marketing and producing the product and the $2 million development costs from $55 million, the net result is $43 million. The net revenues of $21 million and $3 million for the "Medium" and "Low Demand" branches are determined similarly.

First, analyze the "Sell Product Directly" node. It has been determined that there is a 25 percent probability that the demand will be high for the product; a 55 percent probability there will be a medium demand; and, a 20 percent probability the demand will be low. The fact is, the demand will not be any one of these exactly. Rather, it will be something in between—sort of a weighted average of the three, or, more precisely, the expected value. To determine the expected value of revenues for the "Sell Product Directly" node, highlighted in Exhibit 7-11, we use the expected value formula shown previously and repeated here for convenience.

$$EV = \sum_{i=0}^{n} p_i X_i$$

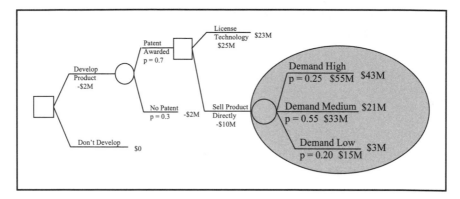

Exhibit 7-11. Research and development decision tree analysis.

Thus the EV for the highlighted potential events is:

$$EV = 43 \times .25 + 21 \times .55 + 3 \times .20$$
$$= 10.75 + 11.55 + .6$$

and $$EV = \$22.9M$$

So the expected value of selling the product directly is $22.9 million, which is only $100,000 less than revenues expected from licensing it. The choices to be considered are several. First, since the differences in expected revenues are so little, the conservative approach is to license the product, avoid the hassle of selling and producing the product, and possibly make $100,000 more. But the second, and very important consideration, is that if the company opts to sell the product directly, then it can keep its employees gainfully employed and still make the same amount of money. A third consideration that must not be overlooked is that EV is not the guaranteed amount of revenues that the product will generate—it is the most likely amount. To make a business decision, one has to consider the worst and best cases. In other words, selling the product directly might not generate but $3 million, but it could generate as much as $43 million. So the decision involves also the amount of risk the organization is willing to take. Assuming a strong project management capability, the best decision is to sell the product directly and work toward marketing and managing for a higher demand.

Developing and Implementing Risk Response Strategies—The Fifth Step

Risk response strategies are the project manager's methods for managing the risk events that occur. A proactive approach to risk management, as with every facet of project management, lessens the impact of those risks that can be identified early in the project's life cycle. Generally, there are four techniques for responding to risks: avoidance, transference, mitigation, and acceptance.

Risk Avoidance

Often the best defense against a risk event is simply to avoid it. We know that risks occur in every project, and it is not feasible, or even wise, to try to structure a project to have no risks. A project without risk is not worth pursuing. On the other hand, facing a risk that is likely to end in loss of time, revenues, or even the entire project, also is unwise. It is also unwise to accept a risk that we have defined as a pure or insurable risk. In these cases, it is best to consider alternative approaches that allow the risk to be transferred or, lacking that, avoided altogether.

The most common way of avoiding a risk is to consider an alternative approach that contains less or no risk. For example, if a system design calls for a new, undeveloped software operating system, it could represent a significant risk to the project. A less risky approach would be to use a proven off-the-shelf operating system, provided that it meets the customer's requirements. A common occurrence in information technology projects occurs during the development of a system that has a specified operating system for which a new version is developed prior to system completion. If the new software version is likely to have defects, it could be better to avoid any attendant risks by continuing with the previous version.

Risk Transference

Risk transference is commonly done in practice by teaming or by hiring a vendor. When the project requires expertise not resident in the organization or group, it is common practice to team with another company or to hire a vendor who does possess the requisite expertise. Common examples of risk transference also occur where insurance is the practical way of planning for risks. For instance, a company that is located in a flood plain or in a tornado alley would routinely purchase insurance against such risks.

Risk Mitigation

Mitigating risk means that the risk event is controlled in such a way that either the impact or the probability of the event occurrence is lessened. Mitigation can occur either by reducing the level of impact, that is, cost or schedule added to the baseline, or by reducing the probability of the event occurring, or both. Generally, mitigation occurs by adding more resources or by using better-trained or more experienced personnel. Using tested and tried technology, rather than newer, untested technology, can also mitigate risk. Risk mitigation is a form of risk acceptance. That is, the risk is expected, and it is an acceptable risk to take; however, an attempt is made to significantly reduce the impact to the project.

Risk Acceptance

Risk acceptance is simply that—the risk is expected, and the level of impact to the project is within the tolerance level of the project team or organization. Usually, this kind of risk is the result of such things as the unpredictability of resource availability. For example, there is always a certain level of risk associated with the real-world problem of sharing resources across multiple projects. A risk to schedule exists if the resources are not available at the time they are needed. In these cases, the risk is recognized and accepted, and it will be dealt with when it occurs.

Implementing Risk Response Strategies

Once a course of action has been developed for a risk event, the strategy must be implemented. A good strategy includes risk triggers to alert the project team of impending risk events. Although the project manager has the ultimate responsibility for the risk plan, she may designate a team member to monitor risk events likely to occur in their technical areas. Monitoring risks involves more than observing whether the anticipated risks occur; it involves determining if the strategies to respond to the risks are adequate or whether other actions are required, which is a function of the next step—tracking risk response.

Tracking Risk Response—The Sixth Step

Tracking risk response is the process of determining whether the planned response strategy is working or whether an alternative approach is needed. It also involves determining if new, unidentified risks occur as a result of implementing response strategies and if the project assumptions are still valid. As a result of risk response tracking, the project may need to be replanned, particularly if the response strategies are not effective, or the original assumptions are not valid.

Controlling Risk—The Seventh Step

Risks are controlled in one of two ways—contingency plans and workaround actions. Contingency plans are plans for implementing risk response strategies. These are plans that can be developed when a potential risk event is identified. Most project risks fall into the category of identifiable risks and are controllable through contingency planning.

Contingency planning usually involves setting aside some level of reserve, usually money but occasionally time as well, to ensure the project is kept on schedule. For example, if a risk is that some critical resources might not be available when needed, the contingency might be to hire a vendor or technical consultants to fill the resource void. Contingencies nearly always require additional funding—hence the need for a contingency reserve.

Workaround actions are activities implemented when the risk could not be foreseen or planned for. These events almost always cost more than the project budget allowed, so the funding is taken from a management reserve. Both contingency and management reserves are established specifically to ensure the project is kept on schedule if a risk event occurs. The basic difference between the two types of reserve is that contingencies are planned into the project budget and are usually controlled by the project manager, whereas the management reserve is not a part of the project budget and is controlled by senior management.

Documenting and Archiving Risk History—The Eighth Step

Neither project managers nor organizations are careful enough about documenting lessons learned and archiving them so that future projects can reap the benefits. The most common excuse is that the team members from a closing project are needed to start new projects and can't be spared for lessons-learned meetings. Ironically, meetings to develop lessons-learned information usually don't take much time since the information, in the form of status reports, audits, and other project paperwork, already contains the pertinent information. Lessons-learned meetings generally take between two hours' and days' time, depending on the size and complexity of the project. If the project manager and team members have maintained a complete project file, the lessons learned information is already available—all that is needed is compilation of the information into a lessons-learned binder. The basic lessons-learned file information includes:

✔ Project name and start and finish date

✔ Key stakeholders such as the project manager, sponsor, task leaders, and customer

✔ Baseline and actual budget and schedule charts

✔ Project issues and their resolution

✔ Identified risks and results of contingency plans

✔ Unidentified risks, their resolution, and project impact

✔ Analysis of team planning and performance

✔ Analysis of metrics collection and usage

✔ Analysis of what went right and what went wrong in the project

Every lessons-learned analysis should be documented and archived with easy access to all project managers and teams. Many companies have begun making these lessons-learned libraries available online to make them even more accessible and effective. But even a hard copy in the organization's resource library is far better than no access at all. Many projects have been saved the problems and costs of reinventing the wheel by having access to workable solutions for risks that continue to reoccur.

Summary

Organizations in general and project managers in particular do not perform risk analyses as well or as thoroughly as they should. Part of the problem is that risks are not easily identified, and, therefore, it is human nature to ignore those things not easily quantified. But the fact is, all projects have risks, and to ensure success, they must be identified and planned for.

Every organization should have in place a risk management process. One model for such a process is contained in this chapter and consists of these steps.

1. Planning risk management
2. Identifying and assessing risk
3. Qualifying risk
4. Quantifying risk
5. Developing and implementing risk response
6. Tracking risk response
7. Controlling risk
8. Documenting and archiving risk history

One of the key factors for risk management success is documenting and using the lessons learned from each project. Without a documented chronicle of what went right, what went wrong, the reasons for both, and the solutions to problems, an organization cannot improve its project success rate. Managing risks is the key to project success.

Chapter 8

Systems Engineering: The Hub of Project Management

Integrating the various elements of a project into a whole system is the crux of a successful project. In the information technology environment, nearly every project is composed of software, hardware, communications, and other components. How these components are integrated into the final product determines whether the project will meet the customer or user's needs, and systems integration depends on a good systems engineering process, the hub of project management. Exhibit 8-1 demonstrates what I mean by this concept. From the graphic, it becomes clearer how the two disciplines, project management and systems engineering management, mesh.

Amazingly, there are a lot of books on project management but few on systems engineering, although systems engineering is done, at some level, on any project having several components, such as IT projects. Fewer still are the books addressing how systems engineering fits into the project management process. Yet it is this discipline that ensures that project components mesh into the final project deliverable. An understanding of systems engi-

183

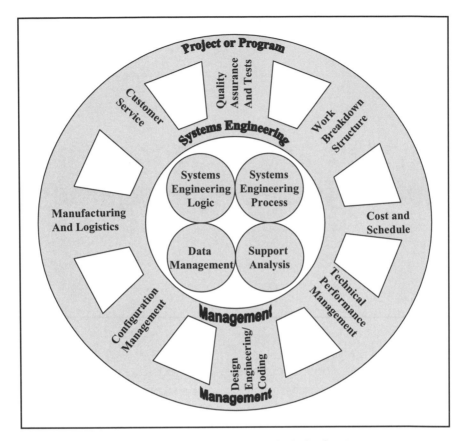

Exhibit 8-1. Systems engineering management is the hub of project management.

neering is crucial to the project manager. Understanding how its tools and techniques apply in the project planning, development, and execution are essential if the project is to be successfully concluded.

Although the systems engineering activities were discussed at a high level in Chapter 3, this chapter addresses the project as a system and describes in more detail how the system is decomposed into its various elements. This chapter also shows how each of these lower elements are planned and developed, how they are individually tracked and controlled, and how they are finally brought together to form the total project deliverable.

The Systems Approach

Defining the "systems approach" is, at times, difficult, but basically it simply recognizes that all the elements of a system must work together, which requires a systematic and repeatable process for designing, developing, constructing, and operating the system. This systematic and repeatable process involves determining the architecture of the system so that, at a minimum, the final design satisfies all the requirements as defined by the customer and agreed to by the provider. The key features of the systems approach are shown in Exhibit 8-2.

The system engineering process is conceptually straightforward and, on the surface, simple. But putting the process in place and executing it can be a significant endeavor because each of these process elements have embedded in them several, and sometimes complex, subelements. A description of each of these elements will aid the understanding of the process.

Requirements Analysis

The requirements analysis process is one that should be continuous. The traditional course of requirements analysis is that stated customer needs are identified, a project plan is developed, and, to

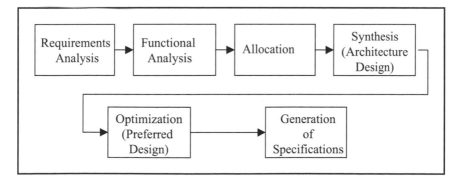

Exhibit 8-2. Key system engineering process elements.

the best extent possible, the project team delivers. The problem with that approach is that the project organization may not have the resources or technical capability to deliver all of the customer's stated requirements. In addition, the customer is very likely to change the requirements anyway as the project progresses, making a matchup of resources and requirements difficult, if not impossible.

Given enough time, a match between a developer's resources and a customer's expectations is eventually met on every project deliverable. The problem is that the matchup often occurs too late in the development process. In other words, projects that unsuccessfully meet their cost, schedule, or performance goals usually are those in which the resources or expectations matchup occurs *after* approval is given to initiate product development. On the other hand, when a customer's needs and a developer's resources are matched *before* product development starts, the more likely the development is to meet cost and schedule objectives.

There are three factors that are key to matching needs and resources before product development begins. First, the developer must employ the technique of systems engineering to identify gaps between resources and customer needs before committing to a new product development. Second, customers and developers have to be flexible. In this instance, flexibility means that the customer needs to be willing to reduce or defer the requirements to future programs long enough so that the developer can make an investment to increase knowledge about a technology or design feature before beginning product development. Third, the roles and responsibilities of the customer and the product developer should be clearly defined and matched to enhance communication and information flow. The objective here is for the developer to be able to significantly influence or even determine product requirements. However, this is done in complete concert with the customer.

When these factors are not present at a project launch, the development of the project deliverable often begins without a match between the developer's resources and the customer's needs. This results in schedule slips and budget overruns.

Functional Analysis

The system functions and subfunctions have to be identified and analyzed. This is the basis for identifying alternatives for meeting system performance and design requirements. Generally, the customer provides at least the high-level functional requirements of the desired product. But a thorough analysis of the customer's stated needs and use or mission of the product will reveal that some of the functions are not needed. Likewise, there are other functions not conceived that should be included in the requirements lists. This process also is an ongoing effort since functionality may change as the development process unfolds. An important result of an ongoing and iterative functional analysis process is that true value engineering can occur. That is, the worth of a required function can be evaluated for possible modifications or deletion.

In the early stages of developing a system, it is best to separate the "how" from the "what" of the system requirements. This approach allows the systems engineer to consider a number of alternative ways to satisfy a requirement, thus optimizing the final solution.

Once the functional analysis is complete, each of these requirements must match a functional element of the system, and vice versa.

Allocation

The primary output of functional analysis is that each identified function and subfunction can be allocated to a set of performance and design requirements. That is, these functions and subfunctions are decomposed in such a way that all the functions and subfunctions and all generic information and data flows among and between them are traceable to a system requirement. If it is determined that a function or subfunction does not support a system requirement, then that function or subfunction is extraneous and has no purpose for the system or the requirement is poorly written.

Synthesis (Architecture Design)

The architectural design of a system is the centerpiece of the total systems engineering process. Simply stated, it is a synthesis procedure that normally requires the formulation of alternative system architectures and a requirements analysis to verify that potential architectures satisfy the stated requirements.

The problem attendant to this step is that one has to define constraints around the acceptable alternatives; otherwise, the job of determining the right solution becomes unmanageable. For example, if there are ten functional areas planned for a system, and there are to be, say, three design choices for each area, then theoretically there are a total of 3^{10} or 59,049 possible architectures. Designing this many alternatives for a system makes no sense, so the typical approach is to narrow the field of possibilities by adding constraints, usually with the input from and approval of the customer. The most common alternative constraints approach is to target a low-cost, minimum effectiveness solution at one end of the spectrum, a high-performance, high-cost solution at the other, and perhaps a third solution midway between the two to start the alternative identification process. The idea is to find a baseline alternative somewhere in between these upper and lower constraints that meets all the system requirements without being unaffordable or too technologically challenging. The end result of this identification process will produce between three and five viable alternatives. Exhibit 8-3 explains how the alternatives are designed against the key functional requirements.

The next step in the process is to determine which of the

System Functions and Requirements	Alternative System Architectures		
	Low-Cost System	Baseline System	High-Performance System
Function 1 Requirement 1.1 Requirement 1.2 Requirement 1.3 Function 2 Requirement 2.1 Requirement 2.2 Requirement 2.3 ⋮ Function N Requirement n.1 Requirement n.2	Describe how each system is designed to satisfy all these requirements to determine a baseline approach.		

Exhibit 8-3. Developing architectures against system functions and requirements.

alternatives offers the best solution to the customer's requirements against the provider's capabilities.

Optimization (Preferred Design)

Once the alternative candidates are defined, a process of evaluating them against each other, using functional requirements to define the evaluation criterion, begins. Usually, a rating system is developed using the customer's stated needs and preferences. For example, the customer may be less interested in cost than performance, in which case the final system may be closer to the upper constraint of Exhibit 8-3. Another desired characteristic of any system is its maintainability. Generally, this is important as an evaluation criterion. Other characteristics that are used as evaluation criteria are meantime-between-failure, guaranteed-in-operation time, or minimum downtime. Whatever the criterion used, each system alternative is evaluated on a scale to determine an overall rating for the alternative. Exhibit 8-4 demonstrates how this evaluation matrix is developed.

Criteria weights are subjective in that the weights and, for that matter, the ratings, are an individual's or team's best guess. However, much of the subjectivity is eliminated, or at least reduced, because all the alternatives are measured against the same criteria. Hence, although this scheme provides no useful results if applied against one system, applying it against several systems provides the best solution in a relative comparison.

Usually, the customer will, through either a brainstorming process or through historical records, or both, determine the evaluation criteria and then rank them according to the importance she perceives each will have in determining the final product. Wherever possible, the provider should be involved with this process because of the expertise that is needed about existing technology, life-cycle cost, maintainability, and so on. When the matrix is developed and each alternative is evaluated, the alternative with the highest score is the one most likely to provide the best value to the customer—best value in this case defined as meeting all the requirements.

Once a decision is made to pursue a particular alternative

Evaluation Criteria	Criteria Weights (W)	Alternative Architectures					
		Alternative A		Alternative B		Alternative C	
		Rating	W × R	Rating	W × R	Rating	W × R
Criterion 1	0.10	9	.90	5	.50	5	.50
Criterion 2	0.08	4	.32	6	.32	8	.64
Criterion 3	0.11	8	.88	4	.44	7	.77
Criterion 4	0.15	3	.45	7	1.05	9	1.35
Criterion 5	0.16	4	.64	8	1.28	6	.96
Criterion 6	0.09	6	.54	9	.81	5	.45
Criterion 7	0.11	9	.99	7	.77	7	.77
Criterion 8	0.10	6	.60	7	.70	4	.40
Criterion 9	0.10	5	.50	5	.50	8	.80
TOTALS	1.00		5.82		6.37		6.64

Exhibit 8-4. Rating alternative architectures.

architecture, the important step of generating specifications for all the subsystems can begin.

Specification Generation

Specifications are usually thought of in an engineering sense, that is, a description of a product reduced to its most basic dimensions and operating parameters. In the IT world, this definition of specifications is valid for most project deliverables, but specification can also describe the functional capabilities of a product. In most instances, it is better to avoid using hard, technical measures in favor of more functional descriptions. In our earlier discussion of statements of work, we pointed out that an SOW is, in fact, a specification.

At this stage of project and product planning, specifications are generated for all the subsystems, regardless of whether the specifications describe precise engineering dimensions, the functional requirements of the system, or both. This step can be an iteration point as well. This is because even though the preferred alternative has been chosen through trade-off and other analyses processes, specification generation often uncovers flaws in the architecture, which may require a modification to the design or even coopting another approach over the preferred one.

These sections described the key elements of the systems engineering process, but what is the relationship of systems engineering and project management? How do the two fit together? Are they completely separate disciplines? The next section answers these questions.

Systems Engineering Management and Project Management

Whether you realize it or not, as a project manager you have been performing some of the functions of a systems engineer—trade-off analysis, systems design, and data management, for example. The question is not so much whether we do systems engineering, but rather, how can we do it deliberately and effectively? The fact that we do some systems engineering intuitively is good, but it is not nearly enough to ensure an optimized solution and a successful project. To be able to more effectively plan and integrate the various components of an IT project, we first need to understand why there is even a need for systems engineering. Then, we must understand how the systems engineering function fits into the overall project management environment.

Why Systems Engineering Management?

Systems engineering management techniques actually rose to prominence during Secretary of Defense Robert McNamara's tenure, to be exact. The problem the DOD had was that programs were becoming more complex and, probably more importantly during that period, more costly. Consequently, the DOD, with Secretary McNamara driving the initiative, began aggressively requiring a formalized approach to defining and defending programs of interest to the different service branches. The initial intent of this effort was to force the services to first accurately define their programs, and second, provide review points that offered possibilities for real go/no-go decisions. The results of formalizing this procedure were that the services complied with the original intent of completely defining their requirements, and the procedure created a whole new way of defining, describing, and managing projects—systems engineering management. Exhibit 8-5 is a depiction of the systems engineering process. For the typical practicing project manager and organization, the problem since then has been: How do you integrate the system's process into the project management environment, and vice versa? Perhaps a better understanding of the philosophy of systems engineering is needed to set the baseline, or point of departure, for discussing how these two disciplines interrelate.

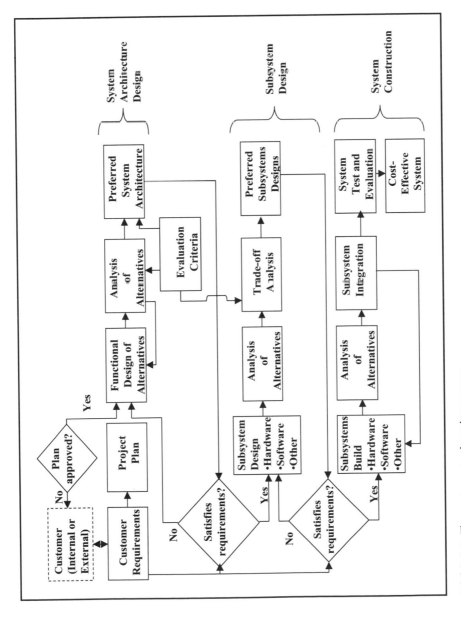

Exhibit 8-5. The systems engineering process.

The Systems Engineering Philosophy

Basically, systems engineering can be described through an understanding of ten propositions (premises) of the systems engineering philosophy, or the systems approach to defining a project's deliverables.

1. *Separation of Problem and Solution.* Traditionally, engineers are incorrigible optimists. In order to generate the enthusiasm needed for tackling seemingly insoluble problems, they have to be. But, at times, this very enthusiasm leads to solutions after only a superficial study of the problem. The purpose of a system's approach to a problem is to first completely define the problem and then, *and only then*, select a suitable solution *after* exploring a number of alternative solution approaches. The primary purpose of systems engineering management is to make it possible to organize and relate system data so that various combinations and permutations of options can be investigated and weighed. The outcome of this process is, hopefully, an optimized solution that provides the best and the most one can get, functionally, for one's dollar at a particular point in time. In optimization, there is a natural tendency to guard against force-fitting a preconceived solution to a problem, based on the strength of a past success with a similar solution. Preconceived solutions stand the risk of becoming either weak solutions or overkill solutions that reduce system effectiveness and/or boost costs.

2. *Defining Systems Definition.* The system definition process should unfold in progressively expanding stages downward, like a pyramid, and not like a uniform cube. Initially, a system is defined in a gross sense; as definition progresses in successively expanding stages, so does the level of understanding and confidence in end-item components and assemblies that make up the total system. Detail definition that is done too soon can lead to the optimization of too many choices on too many levels. This would tend to produce a mass of

data, which might constrain management's vision, confuse, and waste effort, not to mention money.

3. *Responsiveness to Customer's Management Requirements, Not to Procedures.* A provider's internal management practices must be responsive to the customer's requirements, based on the negotiated and tailored approach to fitting or mapping the provider's resources to the customer's requirements. In other words, the procedures in place in the provider's organization have to be flexible enough to accommodate the customer's requirements. Likewise, the customer and the provider have to ensure that the provider's resources sufficiently map to the project requirements, so that the project will be a success, both for the customer and the provider.

4. *Top-Down Approach to Driving Out Packaging of Functional Requirements.* Top-down analysis and packaging of functional requirements, from a total systems perspective down to the lowest component, are practiced by systems engineers to completely define the end products needed to fulfill system requirements. Such an approach ensures attention to detail in progressively expanding stages so that every requirement is accurately identified, accounted for, and mapped to a functional block in the design architecture.

5. *Cost-Schedule-Performance Relationship.* The necessity of controlling the tendency of system costs to grow means that a tight relationship between cost, delivery schedule, and the performance expectations is essential when making realistic trade-offs at every stage of the system design and evaluation.

6. *Constraining a Profusion of Data.* Because the flow of data to stakeholders must be controlled so that the information does not constrain visibility of actual progress—or problems, as the case may be—a tailored process may be required for each individual project. In approaching this problem, it is important to remember that for major levels of decision making, management needs mostly distilled data, but data distilled from conclusive study results and traceable to the customer's

system specifications, i.e., requirements. Thus, only a specifically designed documentation process tailored for the purpose can be traced this way.

7. *Importance of Baseline Control.* After establishment of the baseline, any changes made must fall within the existing defined and agreed scope. This is a gray area between the systems management and project management responsibilities. The systems engineering process is actually the basis for defining the technical baseline of the project, but the project manager's hat requires that the baseline is not violated. Hence, this process is twofold—evaluating changes to the baseline (the function of the systems engineering management process) and evaluating and determining whether the change request is outside the scope (the function of the project management process).

8. *Identification of Respective Responsibilities.* The systems process gets into contractual issues in many ways. One primary responsibility of the systems engineering management function is to positively identify and separate the contractual responsibilities of various contributing entities. Simply stated, this means that if more than one contractor (or vendor) works on a project, the systems engineering process must delineate the responsibility boundaries between the various contributing organizations and the customer. In other words, the responsibilities have to correlate directly with any contract structure, and it is the systems process that identifies this relationship and tracks it.

9. *Understanding Systems Requirements.* The most effective way a contractor or internal provider can prove he understands the customer's system requirements is by making certain that any provided technical data is clearly traceable and responsive to the system requirements. This is one of the fundamental results of a systems engineering process.

10. *Selling System Proposals.* In the earliest stages of a project, one of the first things a provider has to do, or should do, is pre-

pare a proposal—some documentation about how the project will be run and what the technical solutions will be. Hence, it is imperative that a thoroughly reasoned and traceably documented system proposal is prepared for appraisal by several tiers of decision-making hierarchy. And, since these different tiers of decision makers possess varying degrees of technical understanding, the proposal package must contain clear, self-supporting data. The systems process can analyze the system and identify the components, but the challenge is in being able to describe each of these components and the proposed solution in understandable terms.

These are the basic tenets of the systems engineering management philosophy. To be sure, this list is not exhaustive, but to add many more tenets would invite our getting into far more detail than is necessary to make two very important points. First, systems engineering is important to defining and carrying out a project charter, and second, systems engineering and project management are interrelated. They are sister disciplines and competencies. If they are so closely related, how then do they mesh together?

The Relationship of Systems Engineering and Project Management

Systems engineering and project management are separate but closely related functions. In very complex projects it is best to employ a systems engineer, that is, one whose specialty is systems engineering, to perform this function. However, in most typical, even relatively complex projects, it is not uncommon for the project manager and his team to perform the systems engineering function. However it is done, the important point to remember is that to accurately define, implement, and track a project, especially a multifaceted one, it is absolutely crucial that the project manager think in terms of the systems approach.

How these two functions interrelate is actually not so easy to understand because so much of the one function is identical to or overlaps with the other. However, a look at Exhibit 8-6 may explain the relationship, or interrelationship, of the two.

There are several noteworthy aspects of the graphic in Exhibit 8-6. First, notice that I have redrawn Exhibit 8-5, the systems process, so that the systems engineering functions fall logically within the project management activities of a typical four-phased project life cycle. Obviously, there are many internal steps and processes at work within each of these boxes, but I have simplified the graphic to clearly show how the project and systems engineering disciplines work together.

The second thing this graphic should portray is that project management is the overarching discipline throughout the systems engineering life cycle (it might be helpful at this point to refer back to Exhibit 3-2, as well). In other words, systems engineering is the hub of project management, but its use is a means for designing, building, and managing the product. Project management is the means for managing the project, which includes managing the product activities, as well as all other project activities.

The third thing I would draw your attention to is that the system consists of hardware and software, plus other components. The other components include services, human engineering (designing the system for optimal use), training, logistics, and all the myriad bits and pieces that make up the IT system.

One final thing to notice in this graphic is how much effort is required before the system actually gets built. On average, one half of a project budget is spent by the end of the second phase, or before a system is actually at a point to be constructed, tested, and shipped.

Systems engineering activities are, for the most part, activities that are not unfamiliar to us, but few organizations train their project managers or team members in how and why its techniques and disciplines should be applied. A focused, well-trained cadre of project managers and systems people will guarantee a greater project success history.

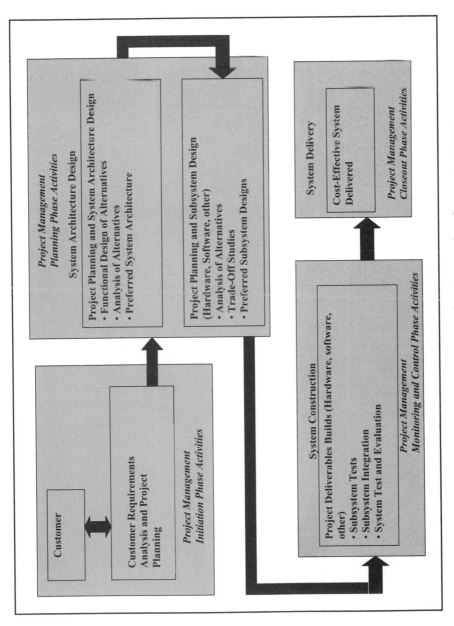

Exhibit 8-6. Relationship between project management and systems engineering management.

Summary

As a formalized discipline, systems engineering management is not very old. It was begun by the DOD in an attempt to force military branches to accurately define their programs and provide review points that offered possibilities for real go/no-go decisions. The result of formalizing this procedure was that the services complied with the original intent of completely defining their requirements. It also created a whole new way of defining, describing, and managing projects.

Systems engineering techniques and systems engineering management are key to the development of optimum project deliverables. Although most project managers are accustomed to using some systems engineering techniques, such as trade-off analyses and developing alternative approaches, there is not a widespread use or even understanding of what systems engineering can do to help the project manager, the project team, and the organization as a whole.

The key features of a systems approach are:

- ✔ Requirements analysis
- ✔ Functional analysis
- ✔ Allocation
- ✔ Synthesis or architecture design
- ✔ Optimization of selection of the preferred design
- ✔ Generation of specifications to start system construction

Implementing these features into every project will guarantee a greater, successful project completion rate.

Chapter 9

Project Monitoring and Control

If the successful project begins with the project plan, as we stated at the beginning of Chapter 6, then the function of monitoring and controlling the progress maintains the successful momentum toward project completion. (Monitoring and controlling a project is imminently easier if the project has been properly planned.) The tools of this phase are well tested and numerous. However, the beginning project manager or new team member is sometimes confused about how the tools are applied for maximum effectiveness and why particular tools are used in particular situations. It is best, therefore, to talk about this phase (sometimes called the implementation phase) as the monitoring and control phase, and to talk about the two components separately.

The first component, project monitoring, is most often done with earned value management (EVM). The description of earned value, how and why it came about, and the mechanics of the earned value evaluation were described in detail in Chapter 2. In this chapter we will talk about how to apply earned value to an integrated project, how to do an analysis, and the consequences of the analysis. The results of the monitoring activities are what we need to control the future direction of the project.

201

The second component, project control, uses our analysis to determine whether anything needs to be done to change how the project is progressing and implements the appropriate measures to get the project back on track, if that is needed.

This chapter expands on the discussion in Chapter 2 about earned value, and it also discusses techniques and tools for getting the project back on track.

Project Monitoring

Earned value management is a term used by PMI to describe the general application of earned value analysis to monitoring project progress. The concept of earned value provides a mathematical way to accurately assess the project's actual progress against the project's planned progress. The DOD, as a way of instituting a standard project analysis and reporting methodology, developed earned value. Fortunately, the earned value methodology not only served the purpose of providing a standard way of reporting project progress to the DOD, but it turned out to be the most accurate, and simplest to use, method for tracking how a project is doing.

There are several earned value formulas that are used to provide different and extremely important cues to the health of the project's progress. It is well worth reviewing these formulas before launching into a practical example and analysis.

Earned Value Formulas for
Monitoring Project Progress

There are three key earned value components that have to be mastered before the earned value methodology can be understood and used. They are the planned value (PV), the actual cost (AC), and the earned value (EV). At this stage, it is easiest to think in terms of tasks than in terms of the whole project. How these costs roll up to the project cost will become evident as we progress in the discussion.

PV is the amount that you estimate the task will cost. It is the amount that you estimate the cost will be for a task's planned schedule, or to say that another way, it is the cost of the scheduled work.

AC is the actual amount of money paid for the work as it progresses. This information comes from invoices paid, labor costs, that is, time sheet data, and materials bought for the task at hand. AC is the actual cost of the work performed on the task.

EV is the amount of money budgeted for the work that is actually performed. This term is the most difficult one to conceptualize because it presents a new way of thinking about progress. The simplest way of think about EV is this: Suppose you have a task that you estimate will cost $1,000 and will take twenty weeks to complete. To simplify the explanation, we will break the task into one-week elements, as shown in Exhibit 9-1.

In the example shown in Exhibit 9-1, I have broken the task into weekly segments to better explain the concept of PV and EV, but especially EV. The total planned value cost of the task is, of course, $1,000, but before the task is completed, the "to date" PV will be determined by adding the costs of the various segments to the assessment point. In this example, we are going to assess the progress at the end of the fifth week. Hence, the PV to date is five times fifty dollars, or $250. If the project were on time, that is, on the planned schedule, then the EV would also be $250. However, in the example we are saying that we are actually ahead of schedule and have completed the equivalent of seven weeks of work. So the EV is the sum of the cost segments actually completed to date, or $350. Another way of calculating EV is to multiply the percentage of workweeks completed times the total task PV ($7/20 \times \$1,000 = \$350$).

With this understanding of the three primary components (PV, AC, and EV) of the earned value management methodology,

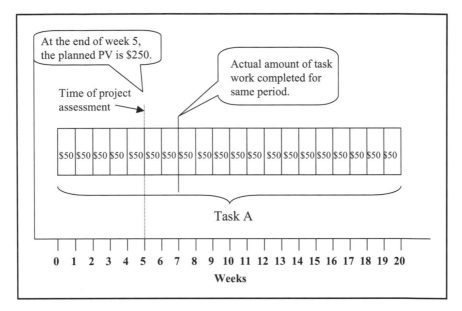

Exhibit 9-1. Determining PV and EV for task work progress.

we can go on to an IT example that shows how to actually monitor the project's progress using earned value.

Monitoring Project Progress with Earned Value Analysis

Earned value analysis is, simply stated, determining how well the
project is doing in comparison with the original plan. The use of
an example best illustrates earned value analysis. Exhibit 9-2 is an
example of an IT project consisting of several tasks. Naturally,
this is only a small representation of a project, but it should suffice
to demonstrate the principles of the technique.

In the example, we have a small IT project that is fourteen
weeks in duration. At the six-week point, we are going to make
an assessment of the project's progress. (Note that the project
manager and his team will have made similar assessments at the

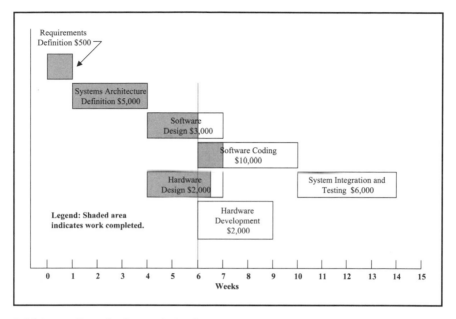

Exhibit 9-2. Earned value analysis of an IT project.

end of each of the previous weeks, but to demonstrate the analysis technique, we are only going to look at the six-week assessment.)

The most convenient way to collect earned value data is in tabular form. Exhibit 9-3 is an example of common earned value tables of the type provided by most project management software programs.

The point of the analysis is to determine whether we are on schedule and on budget. From Exhibit 9-2, it is easy to see that we are actually ahead of schedule. We have completed the work that was planned for completion at the sixth week, we have begun the software coding task, and we have completed more of the hardware design task than was anticipated. However, there is no way to look at this modified Gantt chart and determine whether we are on budget—that has to be done by comparing what is completed against what we have spent. But when we look at the collected data in the earned value table (Exhibit 9-3), the column labeled CV (cost variance) tells the story—we are over budget.

Because the CV is a negative number, we know that the

Earned Value Analysis

Task Name	Col. A % Complete	Col. B Total Task PV	Col. C To Date PV	AC	EV (Col. A × Col. B)	CV (EV − AC)	SV (EV − PV)
Requirements Definition	100	$500	$500	$600	$500	−$100	0
Systems Architecture	100	$5,000	$5,000	$4,500	$5,000	$500	0
Software Design	67	$3,000	$2,010	$2,100	$2,010	−$90	0
Hardware Design	83	$2,000	$1,340	$1,600	$1,660	$60	$320
Software Coding	25	$10,000	0	$3,000	$2,500	−$500	$2,500
Totals		$20,500	$8,850	$11,800	$11,670	−$130	$2,820

Exhibit 9-3. Earned value analysis table.

project is over schedule. Remember that a positive CV indicates an under budget condition, negative indicates over budget, and zero means the project is on budget. Likewise, a positive SV (schedule variance) means the project is ahead of schedule, which is the case in our example. A negative SV would mean the project is behind schedule, and zero means the project is on schedule.

Notice that in the analysis, we have to determine where in the project's development we planned to be at the time of the assessment. We also should know how much work we actually have accomplished to date. The first two tasks, requirements definition and systems architecture design, are completed when we take the assessment at the sixth week. So, at this time, we had planned to spend the money budgeted for the tasks, and we completed the work. So both the PV and the EV for each of the tasks is equal to the amounts estimated, $500 and $5,000, respectively. The next task, software design, is a three-week task, and we planned to have completed two weeks of work at the assessment point. The shaded area indicates that we did, in fact, complete the two weeks, or 67 percent of the work. So we can determine the PV to date and the EV to date by multiplying 67 percent by $3,000, the estimated PV for the task.

The next task, software coding, is a little different—we had not planned to begin that task until the sixth week, or the time of the assessment. So the PV for the task is zero, but the shaded area indicates that we actually managed to begin the work sooner and have finished one week (or 25 percent of the coding) already. Hence, the PV is zero, but the EV is 25 percent x $10,000, or $2,500.

The hardware design task also has gone quite well, and we can see from Exhibit 9-2 that we have completed a half week more work than planned. So the PV to date is 67 percent (2 weeks planned progress divided by 3 weeks total task duration), and the EV is 83 percent (2.5 weeks actual progress divided by 3 weeks total task duration). The other tasks were not planned to begin, and no work has been accomplished on them.

Notice on the earned value table that the totals of PV, EV, and AC can be used to determine the total cost variance and schedule variance for the project as well. Not only does this serve as a check of your math, it also is more meaningful for senior management. After all, their interest is in the project's progress; your interest is in the tasks that are impacting the project's progress.

Other important measures in earned value are the cost performance index (CPI) and schedule performance index (SPI). Because these measures represent the project progress in terms of a percentage rather than a dollar figure, they are important and have more meaning to senior management or to financial people.

CPI is determined by the following formula:

$$EV/AC = CPI$$

So in our example, the CPI is:

$$11,670/11,800 = .99$$

This number can be interpreted to mean that for every dollar we spend on the project, we are getting ninety-nine cents back. If the CPI ratio is less than 1.0, then it indicates that the project is over budget, which is the result we got when we calculated cost variance. But the difference here is that the CPI of ninety-nine cents provides a better relative sense of how bad the situation is. In other words, comparing a cost variance equal to -$130 with a CPI of ninety-nine cents, we know that, although we are over budget, we are actually very close to being on budget. We don't have to make any major changes to the way we are managing the project.

The other measure, SPI, gives a similar indication of how the project is progressing against the planned schedule. The SPI is represented by the formula:

$$EV/PV = SPI$$

So from our example again, the SPI is:

$$11,670/8,850 = 1.32$$

A number less than 1.0 would indicate the project is behind schedule, equal to 1.0 means the project is on schedule, and a number greater than 1.0 means we are ahead of schedule. In this case, we are about 30 percent ahead of where we had planned to be at the sixth week.

These measures, CV, SV, CPI, and SPI are excellent ways to monitor the project's progress. These measures, along with others, are equally good for controlling the project; that is, they can be used to keep the project within acceptable bounds.

Project Control Through Variance Management

The key to controlling a project is using variance management as determined by earned value analysis. One way to use variance management is to determine the acceptable bounds away from the planned budget and schedule that we can tolerate. Generally, about 10 percent variation above or below the planned budget or schedule is about the maximum that can be tolerated. From experience, we know that once a project gets more than 15 percent off its plan, it can not be recovered to more than about 10 percent of the original plan. So the key is to keep the project as close to its original plan as possible, and certainly close enough to recover it, if it does get off track.

Once the bounds are set for the project's budget and schedule, then it is a simple matter to determine how close each task is to its plan whenever an assessment is made. The CPI and SPI measures are perfect for tracking how well the project is doing. Suppose you have a project that has the CPI and SPI values shown in Exhibit 9-4.

Once the CPI and SPI are calculated for each period, it is an easy task to plot them on a chart like the one in Exhibit 9-5. This kind of plotting is easily done in any kind of spreadsheet. Notice that a 10 percent upper and lower limit line has been placed on

Assessment Periods	PV	AC	EV	CPI	SPI
Week 1	$10,000	$10,300	$9,500	.92	.95
Week 2	$6,000	$5,950	$6,250	1.05	1.04
Week 3	$7,500	$7,200	$7,400	1.03	.99
Week 4	$4,500	$4,650	$4,500	.97	1.0
Week 5	$9,250	$9,300	$8,950	.96	.97

Exhibit 9-4. CPI and SPI table for controlling the project.

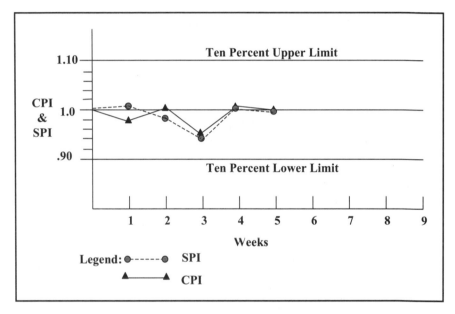

Exhibit 9-5. Tracking CPI and SPI.

the chart. Both CPI and SPI can be plotted relative to 1.0. Remember that 1.0 means on budget and on schedule, so any variation from that point is a potential for concern. However, as long as CPI and/or SPI remain within the 10 percent limits, the project is considered to be progressing according to plan, or at least within acceptable variations from the plan. In our example, the CPI and SPI are close enough to the 1.0 line that there is no need for concern. If it gets off course, it can be quickly brought back onto the planned track. So the example shows a pretty stable and well-run project. However, if all the measurements (either CPI or SPI) are all on the same side of the median line, and if they are slowly getting further away from that line and closer to one of the limits, then the project is clearly going out of control. In that case, there is a need for immediate action to bring the project back on track.

Many inexperienced project managers often question whether it is necessary to have a lower limit, especially for CPI. After all, isn't it a good thing to have a project under budget? Well, maybe. The problem is that being under budget can mean that a task, or a part of a task, is not done or not completed. So any time a project is under budget, it is incumbent upon the project manager to determine the cause. It is just as important to determine why the project is under budget and ahead of schedule as it is to determine why it might be over budget and behind schedule.

Controlling the project also means understanding how the present project status impacts the future project status. This information is determined by two earned value calculations—the new estimate at project's completion and the estimate of money needed to complete the project.

Estimate at completion (EAC) is one number that not only the project team is concerned about—it is also very important to senior management. Consequently, this is one of the numbers that is always requested in status reports.

The EAC is calculated by the formula:

$$BAC/CPI = EAC$$

In this case, BAC is the budget at completion, or the total budget of the project. Returning to the example of Exhibit 9-3, the BAC is $20,500, or the sum of the estimated cost/budget of each of the tasks. The CPI for that example is determined by the formula:

$$EV/AC = CPI$$
$$11,670/11,80 = .99$$

Hence, EAC is equal to:

$$20,500/.99 = \$20,707$$

In this case, the new budget at completion, $20,707, is greater than originally estimated but not by so much that there is a need for concern. In fact, considering that the project is nearly halfway completed, a new estimate of only a little over $200 more than the original estimate is extraordinary—in short, the original estimate was a good one.

Another calculation that is also very important to senior management, and of particular interest to the comptroller, or financial officer, is the estimate to complete (ETC). This number tells the senior management how much money is needed to complete the project. It is important because it is the basis for determining how much cash flow is required until the project is completed.

ETC is calculated with the following formula:

$$\text{BAC (or latest estimate)} - \text{AC} = \text{ETC}$$

In other words, we simply take our latest estimate of the project's cost/budget and subtract the amount of money that has actually been spent to date. In our example, the new EAC is $20,707. The amount of money actually spent to date is found in the table of Exhibit 9-3 and is $11,800. So the ETC is found by the formula:

$$\text{ETC} = 20,707 - 11,800 = \$8,907$$

So to finish the project, we will need $8,907.

All this information is needed to control a project. The controlling process includes not only determining the earned value data, but also reporting it in a way that facilitates controlling it. Progress, or status, reporting provides this important link between analysis and managing the project to maintain the planned budget and schedule.

Status Reporting

A status report is a narrative description of the project's progress, usually provided to senior management and the customer representative on a regular basis, say, each month. The frequency of this report, or any other report, is a function of how complex or risky the project is. Most IT projects are complex and at risk, at least with regards to schedule and technology issues. Thus, it is likely that the project manager will be asked to provide informal reports frequently—even daily—with a formal, written report to follow weekly or, at a minimum, biweekly.

Exhibit 9-6 is an example of a typical status report format, which is designed to provide some very basic information to the reader. In other words, it answers questions like these:

- ✔ What has been done during the reporting period?
- ✔ What problems were encountered and how were they handled?
- ✔ What is going to be done during the next reporting period?
- ✔ Do you expect any problems during the period?

Most senior managers (especially the financial officer) are going to want financial information. Depending upon the organization's sophistication with earned value analysis, you might want to add an earned value report as an attachment. Otherwise, a simple time line showing the budget and the actual expenditures may be sufficient for this report.

Another important aspect of project control is that of managing changes in the project.

Status Report

☐ Project Name: _____ Report Date: _____

Phase: _____ Report Period: _____

Project Manager: _____

Summary of Progress:

Project Issues/Problems/Actions Taken:

Planned Activities for Next Reporting Period:

Milestones:

    Met during this period

    Planned for next period

Financials:
    Report Dates:
        Planned Spending
        Actual Expenditures

Actions/Decisions Pending:

Attachments:

Exhibit 9-6. Sample status report format.

Managing Change in a Project

A documented and functional change control methodology is crucial to project success because so much change is inevitable, particularly in a complex, developing, and evolving IT project.

There are two categories or types of changes the project team and organization need to be aware of and track closely. The first are those changes that the customer initiates as she evaluates the needs. These kind of changes occur because the project requirements were not clear at the start, the technology changes, or the need changes because of market considerations. Sometimes, particularly with new technology or developing technology, it simply is not possible to completely define the project until some design work or prototyping is completed. Whatever the reasons, these kinds of changes constitute changes to the scope and must be accomplished with a change to the contract or, with an internal customer, a formal memorandum of understanding. The reason for a formal change procedure is that most scope changes will impact the budget, the schedule, or both. This category of change should be spelled out in the contract documents and enforced. Otherwise, the project is doomed to suffer scope creep, that is, adding additional tasks onto the project without consideration for the extra costs and schedule time required.

The second category of changes occurs within the project as it develops. These changes are usually those that become evident enhancements, as more of the design and development is understood. They may, or may not, constitute scope changes. This type of change is internal to the project and the organization but, ultimately, requires the customer's consent before implementation.

There needs to be a formalized process for change management that the project team, and all functional personnel, understand and follow because anyone can recommend a product change. Consequently, without a standard change procedure, the project would collapse in chaos. A sample change control procedure is shown in Exhibit 9-7.

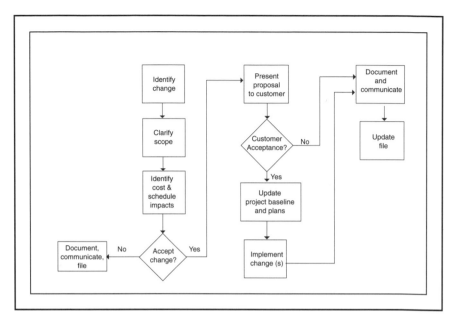

Exhibit 9-7. A sample change control process.

All change requests or recommendations must be directed to the project manager so that they can be tracked, documented, and acted upon. Many organizations authorize their project managers to approve recommended or suggested changes, provided the changes do not impact the budget, schedule, or product performance—that is, no scope impacts. Even then, the project manager actually does not institute the changes without obtaining the customer's approval first.

All potential changes that exceed the project manager's authority are passed on to a change (or configuration) control board (CCB). The CCB is usually a group of three to five members whose function it is evaluate change requests, their viability, and the impact to the project scope. The group usually meets on an ad hoc basis, that is, as needed, but in cases where rapidly or often changing projects are the norm, the CCB may be a standing committee meeting on a regular basis, perhaps once per week.

Changes are recommended by submitting a form describing the change, its impact to the project, how much it will cost in terms of budget and schedule, and its benefits to the product. These changes are not necessarily changes that enhance the product and add to cost and schedule; one can also recommend the elimination of functions, which can substantially reduce both cost and schedule. Exhibit 9-8 shows a sample change request format.

Once a change is approved, the project manager's designated configuration management specialist must document the changes and update the project specifications. In large contracts, the configuration management process is very elaborate and very detailed, with each change documented, numbered with a configuration item number, and logged. The configuration management position is so important that it has become a separate labor category and is considered to be a specialist function.

After the change is approved and the files are updated, the project baseline is updated, the changes are published, and all stakeholders are informed of the changes. Changes to the baseline often—in fact, usually—require a change to the contract. No project changes should ever be approved without an attendant change to the contract.

Even if the customer decides to change the baseline configuration and it is determined that there is no impact on the budget or schedule, a no-cost contract modification should be requested by the project manager. Usually the customer will automatically issue one, but the experienced project manager will always insist on having the modification prior to instituting the changes. These contract modifications are necessary because one of the actions at project completion is to determine whether the goals, objectives, and specifications have been met. Without a contract modification, there is no way to track whether or why a change was made.

Change Request/Recommendation

Project Name: _____ Date: _____

Project Manager's Name: _____ Request Initiated by: _____

Description of the Change:

Reasons/Benefits of the Change:

Impact to Schedule:

Impact to Budget:

Impact to Product Performance:

Attachments (any analysis to support change request position):

Exhibit 9-8. A sample change request form.

Summary

The monitoring and control phase of a project life cycle involves starting the project, monitoring its progress, and controlling day-to-day activities so that variances from the project plan are kept to a minimum.

The key to success in this phase is the monitoring system design. If the project manager and team put into place a systematic way to collect data, analyze the data, control the variances revealed in the analyses, and report the results quickly, the project will progress smoothly. Otherwise the project will be characterized by constant, reactive attempts to put out fires.

Another key aspect of project success revolves around the expertise and efficiency of the team in change management and change control in general. As long as the organization maintains a strict change process and proper procedures, change can be managed. The one major caution in managing change is to ensure that *every* change is implemented *only* after it is agreed to and documented by all stakeholders.

The key tools for this phase of the project are the WBS, Gantt charts, network analyses, earned value analyses, and reporting and change control forms.

Chapter 10

Rapid Development in IT Projects

A component of the monitoring and control phase of the project is its software development methodology. In the earliest stages of planning, a decision about what techniques(s) to be used is made. If schedule is not a concern, then the developing approach is likely to be slower and more deliberate to ensure quality and to ensure that numerous alternative approaches can be explored. If there is an urgency to field a system, then some form of a rapid development technique will be used. Likewise, if the project runs behind schedule, then the rapid development techniques can be employed as a controlling mechanism.

Rapid development techniques are becoming more critical and useful as information technology projects compete in the world market. Some companies seek a special rapid development technique that will significantly improve the project schedule and beat the rush-to-market goal, thus burying the competition forever. Others seek a way to improve schedules so that they can just maintain market share. All companies are seeking ways to improve project performance. Each is looking at rapid development techniques for the answer. But which technique is the silver bullet?

There has been much written on light methodologies during the past five years. Light methodologies refer to techniques that provide processes for significantly decreasing the amount of time spent in the development cycle. These methodologies were developed with a focus on software development, but most are equally applicable to other engineering projects as well. One common problem with the light methodologies is that they all introduce an element of risk into the project. As we saw earlier, risk is not necessarily bad, if it is properly planned for and handled correctly Another problem, at least as viewed by some organizations, is that some of these techniques require extraordinary discipline to properly implement and use, which may not be easy for some individuals or organizations. So the search for and the selection of the right technique is critical and difficult, particularly when the right technique might just be an improvement in the organization's existing processes.

This chapter discusses the dimensions of rapid development in order to provide a basis of understanding about the project elements that can be modified to improve the development process, and it provides a strategy for making these improvements. It also discusses how to determine whether a rapid development technique, in the sense of a light methodology, is needed at all. The chapter also discusses some common development models and how they can be enhanced to improve development schedules. It ends with a discussion of the better-known rapid development techniques and light methodologies and the advantages and disadvantages of each.

The Dimensions of Development Speed

According to Steve McConnell, there are four dimensions, or components, that impact development speed.[1] If any or all of these dimensions can be improved, the development schedule is likewise improved. The four dimensions are:

1. Process

2. People

3. Product

4. Technology

These four dimensions apply in every project, in every industry, and in every organization. The obvious, but often not recognized, solution then would be to examine each of these four dimensions and to change those that are adversely affecting the project. The problem is that we often opt for some magic solution to our problems rather than recognizing our weaknesses and correcting any problems. However, each dimension has associated with it a number of common problems that can seriously impact any project. Recognizing these problems (and some possible solutions) could significantly improve your schedule and your company's competitive position.

Process

Every organization has processes for developing software or their other project tasks. The processes may be informal, that is, not documented or rigorously followed, or they may not be current.

Every organization should have documented guidelines for each of the processes supporting the project. Some common processes include:

- ✔ Developmental fundamentals (a process for establishing a development methodology)
- ✔ Quality management (a process for identifying and implementing quality standards and assessing the product's quality against them)
- ✔ Risk management (a process for identifying, assessing, and controlling the project risks)

Every organizational process should be examined and reengineered for currency and effectiveness. Rigorously recording and implementing lessons learned from each project that passes through the system should constantly improve them.

People

The human side of project management is often its most challenging element. Compared with managing people, technical problems are relatively easy.

There are several key factors a project manager should consider when forming and managing the team. They are:

✔ Skilled talent
✔ Job matching
✔ Career advancement
✔ Team balance
✔ Misfit elimination

Skilled Talent

Too many projects fail or suffer because the team members are not the best for the job. Many project managers approach functional managers with requests for personnel without indicating the specific individuals she would like to have on the team. The most important skill of a successful project manager is the ability to negotiate. Considering that the project manager generally must negotiate for everything—budget, personnel, capital equipment, more time, and so on—it is not surprising that the more successful ones have highly developed negotiating skills. To ensure that the project team is composed of the best talent, the project manager must approach functional management and request specific individuals. The individuals requested may not be available to work on the project, but having asked for them by name immediately establishes the experience, education, and capability level the project manager needs. So, rather than supplying someone who happens to be available at the moment, the functional manager is more likely to attempt to replace the requested individual with someone who has as good or better qualifications.

Job Matching

Forcing someone into a job she is not qualified for, or not happy doing, is sure to result in a team member who is dissatisfied and even detrimental to the project. As obvious as that statement is, it is not difficult to find team members who are ill suited for their positions or performing tasks they detest. A good leader will recognize the importance, not only to the team member but also to the project, of matching each person with the right job. However, job matching means more than assessing skills; it also means assessing personalities and preferences. Using standard assessment tools such as the Myers-Briggs Type Indicator is a good way to determine team member preferences in terms of whether a person likes working alone or in a group, working at tasks requiring attention to detail, or whether he might be a better planner than a developer. Whatever the process used, the likelihood of project success improves significantly with team members whose skills, experience, and preferences are matched to their assigned jobs.

Career Advancement

To the best extent possible, every project experience should be one that enhances the team member's potential for advancement. Helping the team member self-actualize will gain the project a loyal, dedicated, and highly productive worker and will help the organization in training its future senior management.

Career advancement in the context of project management has taken on a new meaning since project management came to be viewed as a legitimate career path during the late 1980s and early 1990s. Before that time, project management was a respected job description. However, to progress up the corporate ladder, one typically had to take either the marketing and new business development or financial path. Today project management is recognized as a career path in its own right. Project managers have a much broader knowledge base about company operations than do most functional managers. This is particularly true in those organizations that encourage project managers to attain the project management professional (PMP) certification. Many organizations are providing their project managers and team members with additional project management training. Some companies are requiring that their employees be certified before they can even become project managers.

Team Balance

Team balance means that the each team member's skills, knowledge, and experience must complement every person on the team. For example, if one team member is an exceptional software developer but a poor communicator, another team member with strong communication skills might be assigned to translate the developer's progress into reports, briefings, and status reviews. Not only must the team's technical skills and knowledge be balanced, but it also needs to have balance in the way the team members interrelate with each other. Maintaining team balance is more challenging for the project manager than solving technical problems in the project.

Misfit Elimination

Though a difficult and unpleasant task, eliminating team members who do not pull their weight, or who cannot get along with the other team members, is crucial to any project's success. Too often, project managers allow a problem to fester because they do not like confrontation, they want to give a person another chance, or they simply do not know how to handle the situation. Nevertheless, a key leadership requirement for the project manager is to know how and when a misfit must leave.

The project manager faced with a misfit on the team should try to determine the root cause of the problem, and she should try to resolve any issues. All conflict issues must be addressed immediately as they occur, and a reasonable time should be allowed for correction of the problem. But for the good of the team, project, and organization, the project manager must be decisive and expeditious in bringing any issue to a final and clean solution. This includes eliminating team members.

Product

This dimension, arguably the most damaging to development speed and perhaps the hardest to control, has to do with the project deliverable or product. If the development speed is to be improved, two characteristics of the product need close attention—the size and the complexity.

Failed projects typically have one recurring characteristic—they are very large, or they are large relative to the size of the organization's capability. Software developers in particular have no fear about attacking products (i.e., project deliverables) that are designed to perform myriad functions. However, more functions require greater, and longer, efforts.

The product is the most tangible part of the project. It offers the best opportunity for making changes that will favorably impact the schedule. The size of the product in terms of cost to develop and build, numbers of resources required, and time to complete may be beyond the organization's capability to perform, even if the product represents the organization's core business. To control the size of the product, the organization can either team with other organizations and approach the project from the perspective of a larger entity, or the product can be divided into manageable pieces, options, or phases.

In terms of functionality, the complexity of the product is

also troublesome for most organizations. Engineers are notorious for adding functionality to a product, even when it is not specified. But added functionality begets added effort. It has been estimated that cutting the functionality of a medium-sized product in half reduces the effort required to complete it by two-thirds. In other words, for every function added, effort increases exponentially.

Development speed can be greatly improved by controlling the product size and complexity.

Technology

There are two aspects of technology that impact development speed—rapidly changing technology that makes the product obsolescent before it is introduced into the market, and changing old technological tools for new ones.

We can control the first problem, rapidly changing technology, by being circumspect in the choices made during product design. If the technology is unpredictable, relative to when it is liable to change, then an alternative design is in order. However, it is also the case that technology changing in the middle of a product development cycle can be worth the risk, depending upon the business benefits of the change and how well it is planned and controlled.

The second aspect of technology change, changing old tools for new, is predictable and can significantly improve development speed. We simply mean that existing software design, development tools, and equipment need to be examined periodically to ensure that the project team is using the most effective and efficient tools available.

Having considered the four overarching dimensions that impact development speed, it is possible to develop a general strategy for implementing a rapid development process into the team's working environment.

A General Rapid Development Strategy

The term "rapid development strategy" conjures up images of applying new and exotic techniques to the development process. The fact is, most processes can be significantly improved just by making them more efficient. Improving development schedules is no exception. The best strategy for rapid development is one that focuses on these four points:

1. Avoid classic mistakes.
2. Apply developmental strategies.
3. Manage risks to avoid catastrophic setbacks.
4. Apply practices that are oriented toward schedule improvement.

The first three points are those that any efficient developer would follow and should be common practice. However, organizations tend to ignore the obvious in favor of the silver bullet, which, sad to say, does not exist. But if the first three points are combined with the last bullet, which refers to three specific schedule enhancement techniques, the overall development process will be improved and shortened.

Avoiding Classic Mistakes

Organizations and project teams make a number of mistakes that have direct and dire impacts on development schedules, in particular, and on productivity, in general. Although there are many more common mistakes than are presented here, I have listed the four or five in several categories that seem to be the most prevalent.

People

    ✔ Lack of stakeholder buy-in. (This is usually the result of a poor stakeholder process or no stakeholder management process.)

✔ Unrealistic expectations. (They are often the result of promises made by the organization to the customer in order to secure the business.)

✔ Heroics. (A result of the inclination of project managers, or team members, who state their ability to accomplish unrealistic project goals in order to please senior management or customers.)

✔ Uncontrolled problem employees. (This mistake occurs when functional, or project, managers are unwilling to eliminate employees who don't fit in the organization.)

✔ Adding people to a late project. (This is a time-honored management technique to attempt to recover schedules. It often works in engineering and construction projects but has the opposite affect in IT projects, principally because of the learning curve.)

Process

✔ Overly optimistic schedules. (This occurs when an organization commits to an unrealistic schedule to improve a competitive position.)

✔ Insufficient risk management. (Risk management is one key project management function that is not generally done well. Too few organizations have well-developed risk management processes that support a proactive approach to potential risk events.)

✔ Insufficient planning. (Approximately 50 percent of the IT project schedules should be consumed with the planning and design processes. Instead, the tendency is to rush into the coding mode before planning is complete, sometimes before it is even begun.)

✔ Abandonment of planning under pressure. (Even when adequate planning has been accomplished, the tendency is to abandon the plan when things don't go well or when the project falls behind schedule.)

Product

✔ Requirements gold plating. (This often results when the seller attempts to give the customer more than he asked for. It usually ends with implied functionality, as opposed to contracted functionality, attempts by the seller to collect for work not originally requested, attempts by the buyer to obtain functionality not requested but implied, or all the above.)

✔ Feature/scope creep. (This usually results from the seller's desire to please the customer, that is, agreeing to small changes in the product without a documented change to the scope. One, two, or a few changes without a corresponding scope change usually are inconsequential to the schedule or budget. The cumulative effect of several such changes can destroy the project.)

✔ Developer gold plating. (Many developers and engineers are guilty of adding functionality to a product just because they discover a functional possibility as they develop the product. Even if the added function is a good idea, the schedule and budget will probably suffer if the customer does not formally approve the change.)

✔ Research-oriented development. (Products or subsystems that require research are not development projects—they are research projects. Attempting both in the same project inevitably results in longer schedules and more spending.)

Technology

✔ Silver bullet or magic bean syndrome. (Because of the rush-to-market requirement in IT, looking for one exotic solution to all the development problems is common and disastrous. Only sound, documented, implemented, and supported development strategies will improve the development process.)

✔ Overrated new tool and methodology savings. (This mistake is related to the silver bullet syndrome. It occurs when organizations buy the latest fads in tools or techniques in the hope that they will resolve any development or productivity problems.)

✔ Tools switching. (Once a project has begun, the tools used for development of the project deliverables should never be changed during development unless the swap-out was scheduled in the project plan, or unless the tools prove to be completely inadequate.)

✔ Lack of automated source-code control. (Uncontrolled source-code changes are still one of the most serious reasons for project failure. Change and conversion control processes are crucial not only for source-code but for scope and configuration as well. Without them, the project is doomed.)

Classic mistakes occur because they become so common that they are transparent in the work environment. As obvious as they might seem, classic mistakes must be identified, planned for, and eliminated. The result will be a significantly shortened schedule.

Applying Developmental Strategies

There are several fundamental strategies associated with development that also can improve schedules. Like the classic mistakes, most of these fundamental strategies are obvious. But like the mistakes, they are too obvious to notice without a conscious effort. The following strategies are categorized to focus attention on functions within the organization that need strengthening.

Management Fundamentals

✔ Schedule and budget estimating. (Nearly all schedules and budgets are underestimated because the organization does not have good estimating techniques and processes in place, does not support them if they do have them in place, and does not train people in the art and science of estimating. Another major problem is that senior management too often arbitrarily reduces the estimates for fear a contract can't otherwise be successfully completed.)

✔ Planning. (The planning function should consume nearly half of the project schedule, but because of the pressure to rush-to-market or because of senior management pressure to show progress, the tendency is to forget planning and start coding.)

✔ Tracking. (Project control is dependent upon a good tracking methodology and process. This process must include scope and configuration change management systems that are rigorously implemented and followed.)

✔ Measurement. (Measuring progress and measuring metrics are key to current and future project successes. Measuring progress means that the project management organization has in place methods, tools, and techniques for tracking the project tasks and for measuring variation from the established baseline. Measurements of metrics, such as numbers of defects, defect removal rates, or errors in coding, are needed for the project team to measure system quality and progress and to improve the estimating techniques for future projects.)

Technical Fundamentals

✔ Requirements management. (The failure to completely identify, fully develop, or properly manage project requirements is the single most cited reason for project failure. Requirements management includes determining exactly what the customer wants and then managing any changes that occur during the life of the project.)

✔ Design. (Too often the coding begins before there is a design. System design, like planning, is an activity in which discernible progress is difficult to show. Consequently, the tendency is to rush into metal bending and software coding because these are the activities that, on the surface at least, demonstrate progress. On the contrary, inadequate design always increases the schedule.)

✔ Construction. (System construction techniques designed to improve schedules should include testing at key points. The most effective software development projects tend to be those in which the developers write test plans and run the tests as they are developing the code. This approach encourages testing in small increments that are easily and quickly corrected as defects are found, thus improving the overall development schedule.)

✔ Software configuration management. (One of the most critical, but poorly accomplished, functions in software development projects is managing configuration changes. Generally, we think of configuration changes in two different ways. First, configuration changes can be changes to the product as it is being designed or constructed— essentially changes to the scope or original concept. Second, configuration changes might mean different functionality for the same basic product. That is, the basic system might have a certain memory capacity and speed, but another customer might request the basic system functions but with a higher memory and speed capability. In any case, tracking, controlling, and managing changes to the system is required to optimize the schedule.)

Quality Assurance Fundamentals

✔ Error-prone modules. (These are modules that, because of poor design, inattention to code-writing fundamentals, or overly complex routines, have an inordinate amount of errors. Isolating these modules and quickly correcting them will improve the schedule and strengthen the overall design. Usually, the error-prone problem resembles the 80/20 rule, which states that 80 percent of the problems are caused by 20 percent of the modules.)

✔ Testing. (Quality assurance relies on testing and other forms of inspection to determine the viability of the design and development. Testing often throughout the development, construction, and implementation stages will result in fewer defects and faster convergence to product completion and customer acceptance.)

✔ Technical reviews. (These are reviews to determine how the overall project is progressing relative to the plan. They also track how individual tasks are progressing according to requirements and design. A balance must be struck between having technical reviews often enough to ensure product integrity and so often as to interfere with the project progress.)

✔ Quality design. (Designing quality into a system and not inspecting it is by now the mantra followed by all who strive for high-quality products. Traditional quality processes depended heavily on quality inspection of the finished product, which often led to scrapping parts and reworking the product, a practice that can increase schedule and costs. Designing quality into the product from the project start, on the other hand, substantially reduces the need for rework, and generally improves the finished product. An equally important consideration is simplicity. Software developers know the importance of simple designs and simple routines and how much they improve their schedules, not to mention frustration and stress levels. In general, the objective in coding and software development should always be to use the simplest approach, routine, or coding sequence that works and satisfies the requirement. Anything more raises the potential for errors or defects.)

Managing Risks to Avoid Catastrophic Setbacks

The importance of risk and risk management were discussed in detail in Chapter 7. However, it is worth restating. Risk management is a developmental strategy that protects the project, and the organization, from failure. If properly exercised, it also carries with it the collateral benefit of significantly improving the development schedule. When one considers how devastating an unplanned risk can be, it is a wonder that risk management is not the highest priority of every organization. Risk management is a process that has to be supported by senior management, documented and promulgated to everyone in the organization, and implemented without fail in every project. To do less is to invite failure.

One cannot plan for, or identify, all risks. As we have pointed out, there are simply some risks that are not known, nor can their impact to the project be anticipated. But the majority of risks can be anticipated and planned for with contingency plans and reserves, either in money or time. The other risks can be dealt with if they occur, provided the organization is oriented toward proactively meeting and dealing with them.

One key component of risk management that is often overlooked, even in reasonably astute organizations, is the identification of risk triggers. A risk trigger is an event or an indication that signals the likelihood that a risk event is about to occur. If the project team has identified triggers, they can then recognize the potential onset of the risk event before it happens, and they often are able to eliminate the risk.

The three components of a rapid development strategy discussed to this point are really nothing more than efficient development practices. In other words, they are practices that any good software development organization should already practice. However, even good development organizations need to reexamine their processes occasionally, make sure their procedures are current, and make sure that the project teams are practicing them.

Improving on basic development practices will improve the developmental process, but adding practices that target schedule improvement directly will shorten the development schedule even more.

Applying Schedule-Oriented Practices

Indirectly attacking the schedule by avoiding classic mistakes, applying developmental strategies, and managing risks definitely shorten the development time, but the amount of improvement depends entirely upon the amount of process or procedural improvement needed. In other words, organizations that already practice efficient development and continually improve their procedures will not realize much, if any, improvement in the development schedule simply by fine-tuning their methods. However, there are other, more direct schedule-oriented practices that significantly improve development time, even for those already efficient organizations. These schedule-oriented practices do not, however, take the place of good, efficient development techniques; they are used to enhance them.

There are three basic categories of schedule-oriented practices: speed-oriented practices, risk oriented practices, and visibility-oriented practices. The first (speed-oriented) means exactly that—concentrating on those practices that directly increase the speed of development. The second category has to do with focusing on risk elimination to avoid any kind of delay that might impact the schedule. And the third category focuses on those practices that provide complete project visibility to the customer and other stakeholders, thus avoiding delays due to misunderstandings, misinterpretation, or miscommunication.

Speed-Oriented Practices

Speed-oriented practices are techniques that shorten the development schedule but generally add risk. These techniques add risk when they involve either accomplishing tasks in parallel that might otherwise be done serially, or they involve developing project requirements with the customer as the project progresses, or both. Conscientiously adding risk to a project is not necessarily bad, but it does require diligence, tracking, and a contingency plan.

An example of applying a speed technique is shown in Exhibits 10-1 and 10-2. Exhibit 10-1 shows a partial project following a typical waterfall development process, that is, the phases or tasks follow each other serially. Exhibit 10-2 shows the same project being expedited by overlapping the tasks. Beginning work on the next task before its predecessor is complete shortens the development schedule. However, by starting the next task, one has to make assumptions that may not be correct. Hence, an element of risk is interjected into the process. The less stable the requirements, the less such an approach should be used. Dealing with more assumptions only exacerbates the problem of undefined requirements.

Scheduling Risk-Oriented Practices

In general, risks invariably affect the schedule. Some risk events affect the schedule more directly and with more force than others

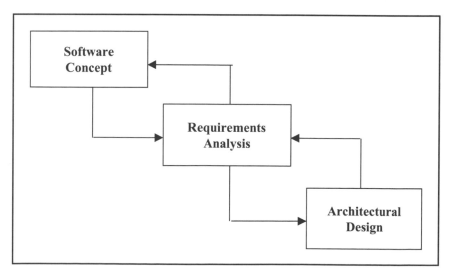

Exhibit 10-1. Partial example of waterfall development.

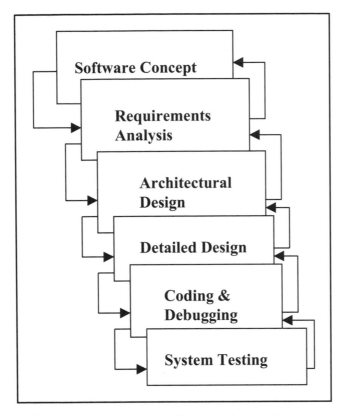

Exhibit 10-2. Example of a modified waterfall development.

do. For instance, a project having tasks that require special skills represents a threat to the schedule, if the appropriate resources are not available when needed. So a risk-oriented strategy would be to determine what skills are needed and when they are needed, then arrange for the requisite resources—either by teaming with a specialty company, hiring consultants, or even opting for an alternative technical approach, thus avoiding the skill set crisis.

Risk-oriented practices have more to do with avoiding delays than speeding up an existing development process. But the more sensitive a project team and organization is to risk, the fewer risk-related delays will occur, creating a faster and smoother development cycle.

Visibility-Oriented Practices

It is often the case that customers and other stakeholders delay projects when they try to satisfy their own needs, or requirements, for information or status. This situation is particularly prevalent in projects that are of strategic importance or that have critical impact on the future of the organization, such as a new product with the potential for creating a competitive or market edge. Applying practices that provide visibility into the project activities and project progress satisfies the customer's or stakeholders' needs. In addition, it improves the schedule by eliminating unplanned reviews and inquiries. It also provides the added benefit of securing customer and stakeholder support and help throughout the project life cycle.

It is not likely that you will employ one or the other of these three schedule-oriented practices. It is more likely that you will use a combination of the three, because focusing on only one practice (to the exclusion of the others) generally creates problems in the other two areas. For instance, concentrating on speed invariably introduces some risk. So an approach that increases development speed, introduces a moderate, but controllable, amount of risk, and actively includes stakeholders leads to a faster and smoother development schedule.

Light Methodologies

Light methodologies are so called not because they are less effective nor applied to simple development efforts. They originally came to be known as "light" methodologies because they were developed, in part, to eliminate much of the documentation that strangles traditional techniques. In other words, they are meant to be less bureaucratic.

Light methodologies are relatively new, having been developed within the last five to six years. Some of these techniques are receiving wide use in the IT industry because they do significantly increase development speeds. However, as with every technique, none are perfect. Each has its own shortcomings.

Although there are several light methodologies in use, we will discuss only a few to provide an understanding about what they are meant to do, compared with traditional techniques, and to round out the discussion about rapid development in general. With this introduction to light methodologies, it is hoped that you can begin to formulate ideas about how to improve your own development schedules and processes. But some words of caution: The best approach is not going to be one of these techniques alone—it is going to be the application of good development practices in conjunction with some of the other rapid development techniques and, perhaps, a variant of these light methodologies.

Extreme Programming

Extreme programming (XP) has received the most attention of all the light methodologies. This popularity is due in large measure to Kent Beck who is the principal author of the technique. Mr. Beck also has a remarkable ability to draw attention, meant in the most positive way, and the ability to entice others to use XP in their work. The fact that he introduced XP into a large, highly visible, and troubled project (Chrysler's C3 payroll project) and saved it from near certain failure made the technique a household word, at least in the software community. To some extent, the technique has been so popular that it has overshadowed many other equally effective techniques.

XP is a very disciplined process, which is both its strong and its weak point. The discipline is its strong point because any disciplined process is better than many of the chaotic practices that too often exist in software development. The particular discipline of this technique eliminates many common problems such as risks and testing issues. The disadvantage of the methodology is that many software developers find the process too rigid and find that they cannot function as well or as creatively. Therefore, whether the technique should be applied depends on how effectively the project manager leads the effort and whether the team can operate under such rigorous guidelines.

These practices are woven into the XP process so that each supports the others. The technique, as do all these light methodologies, depends heavily on communication and feedback, especially with the customer but also with the other stakeholders. The strongest point of the technique is that it requires the developer to write test plans as he is coding and then to test the code at short intervals. This testing approach results in a continuous integration and build process that yields a very stable platform.

Extreme programming is an evolutionary process that iterates into a basic, and very stable, platform. Another key element of XP is simplicity—simplicity of design and simplicity of coding. A major objective of XP development is to incorporate the simplest programming and routines possible that will satisfy the requirements, resulting in faster development and fewer defects. In addition to being its best and best-known champion, Kent Beck has also written the best reference book on the subject—*Extreme Programming Explained: Embrace Change.*[2]

The Crystal Family of Light Methodologies

In the early 1990s, Alistair Cockburn began working on methodologies at IBM. Mr. Cockburn's approach was to take some of his own experience and marry that with the experiences of other project managers who had tried (or were in the process of trying) to improve development processes. The result is not a single methodology but rather a family of methodologies to accommodate different project types and complexities. The Crystal family of methodologies is designed with the view that most people do not work as well with highly disciplined methodologies such as XP. So although Crystal methodologies are heavily oriented toward people and communicating (just like XP), they are not as productive; Cockburn opted to trade off productivity for ease of use.

The key element of the Crystal family is that the methodologies are iterative and designed to help people find and correct mistakes early.

Feature-Driven Development

The object-oriented community developed the concept of feature-driven development (FDD). Basically, FDD focuses on short iterations that deliver tangible functionality. These iterations typically occur in two-week intervals.

Feature-driven development is built around five processes. They are:

1. Model the system.
2. Develop a system features list.
3. Plan the project by system feature.
4. Design the system by feature.
5. Build the system by feature.

The first three processes are done at the beginning of the project, essentially planning the work, and the last two processes are actually doing the work.

To accomplish the work, there are two types of developers assigned. One type is the class owner and the second is the chief programmer. The chief programmer is the more experienced developer and is responsible for building the features assigned to him. The chief programmer identifies the classes associated with his features and makes up a team of those class owners to develop the assigned features. Basically, the chief programmer is the lead designer and mentor while the class owners do most of the feature coding.

Open Source

Open source is a well-known style of software, but because the open source community has definite ways of doing things, there are lessons to be learned that are applicable to rapid development.

In an open source environment, there is usually one person who maintains the software. Others can make coding changes, or they can add code to a basic system, but it is done through patch files fed to the maintainer. The maintainer reviews the changes or additions, approves them (or not), and adds the changes to the basic system as appropriate. The key point in this approach is that only one person can make changes directly to the system, which protects the integrity of the system and facilitates configuration and version changes.

All the light methodologies have an adaptive nature to them. One major benefit of these techniques is that the design can be changed or fine-tuned as it evolves. One of the problems in software development is that the value of the software cannot really be assessed until it is complete and in use. It is often difficult, or impossible, to completely define the system requirements before starting an IT project. So using an adaptive process allows the developer and the customer to jointly develop the requirements as the project progresses.

Summary

Rapid development techniques are of interest to everyone in the software and IT industries because of the rush-to-market pressure and because of the changing nature of technology. However, too many organizations expect to find the silver bullet that will cure all their development ills. Unfortunately, there are no silver bullets, but there are many ways to improve the development schedule.

The most effective and efficient way to improve development schedules is to apply a strategy that:

✔ Avoids classic mistakes.

✔ Applies developmental strategies.

✔ Manages risks to avoid catastrophic setbacks.

✔ Applies schedule-oriented practices.

There are several techniques known as light methodologies that have been developed during the last five to six years that significantly improve the development process. But they are more effective when used in conjunction with fundamental improvement of the organization's processes.

Notes

1. Steve McConnell, *Rapid Development: Taming Wild Software Schedules* (Redmond, Washington: Microsoft Press, 1996).
2. Kent Beck, *Extreme Programming Explained: Embrace Change* (Reading, Massachusetts: Addison-Wesley Publishing Company, 1999).

Chapter 11

Principles of
Project Closeout

Project closeout is often the most difficult phase of a project, not because the project is coming to an end and the customer and your senior management expect the project to have been completed on time, on budget, and in accordance with the customer's requirements, although that is certainly important. The difficulty is mostly created because of the draw upon your resources to other projects. Functional managers have enormous pressures to support every project in the organization. Generally, an organization never has as many resources on staff as it needs to support the projects it pursues, and that is as it should be—it is a function of efficient resource utilization. That fact notwithstanding, there are never enough resources to go around, so functional managers are constantly seeking ways to siphon off resources from one project to apply against another project's needs. Consequently, project managers feel that they are losing their resources before the project work is completed—and that is usually an accurate assessment. So what can a project manager do to successfully close out her project? That is what we are going to explore in this chapter.

Activities of the Closeout Phase

The project manager's function is largely administrative during this phase of the project. It is the time to ensure that all the requirements have been met, the product is delivered and working, all bills are paid, all invoices are sent, the project office is properly closed, and all team members are assigned to new jobs. But "administrative" does not mean that the task is easy.

Ideally, the project team starts planning for the project closeout no later than the beginning of the development phase of the project life cycle. The planning should be done even earlier if there is enough information available, but it often is not practical to develop a closeout plan until there is a clear understanding of all the project and product requirements. In any event, a closeout plan should be in place before the product development begins. Exhibit 11-1 is a sample of a WBS of closing activities. The following checklist, Exhibit 11-2, and the subsequent discussion take a closer look at the closeout activities.

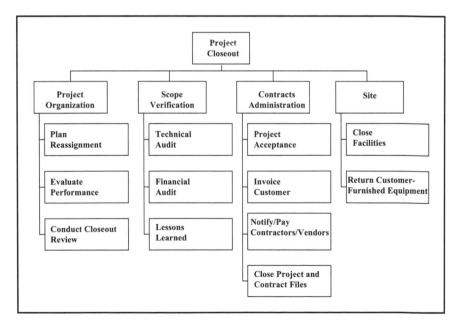

Exhibit 11-1. A WBS for the closeout phase.

1. Scope verification
2. Financial audit
3. Product completion and delivery
4. Customer sign-off
5. Contract closeout
6. Project office closeout
7. Lessons learned
8. Personnel reassignment
9. Close and archive files
10. Prepare for product maintenance

Exhibit 11-2. Activities for closing out a project.

If all the closeout activities are completed, the project manager and his team will have completed a major task.

Scope Verification

A favorite question on PMI's Project Management Professional (PMP) certification examination is: When does one conduct scope verification? The natural (but incorrect) answer is during scope development. Of course, you verify the scope is correct and complete during the scope definition and development process, but scope verification comes at the end of events—tasks, phases, and the project. The objective is to ensure all the scope requirements for that event, whether a task, phase, or the project, are accomplished.

Scope verification constitutes one of the two audits, the technical audit, which is conducted during this phase. The second audit is to determine the project's financial status.

The Financial Audit

The purpose of the financial audit is obvious—you want to know if all the bills are paid and all the invoices have been sent out. But you also need to know another important piece of information. Namely, how well did the actual expenditures match the planned budget?

An often overlooked benefit of a financial audit is the opportunity to collect metrics that can be used to improve the cost estimates. Estimating techniques can be improved every time a project is accomplished by using the variances between the planned budget and actual costs to refine estimating methodology. At the minimum, these variances can be used as weighting factors to adjust new project estimates.

Product Completion and Delivery

Naturally, the primary objective of the project is to complete the customer's product. Basically, the product is completed at the end of the implementation phase, but there still are some final tests and clean-up chores required before the product can be delivered. Most often, acceptance is contingent upon a successful acceptance test, or simply stated, a demonstration that the system works as advertised. If so, the final step is delivery and installation of the system, which, incidentally, may come before the acceptance demonstration. In other words, it is not uncommon to install the system and then conduct the final tests in front of the customer.

Customer Sign-Off

One of the crucial elements of any contract, external or internal to the organization, is a clear explanation of the acceptance criteria. All of us probably have experienced projects that seem to have no end. Usually, this phenomenon occurs because there are no stated acceptance criteria that the customer can use to determine whether the product or system is completed. If there are no criteria, then the customer can always aver that the product does not meet the requirements.

The customer's sign-off literally means she agrees that you

have indeed developed the system to specification, i.e., requirements, and that it is accepted. If the project resulted from an
external contract, sign-off may be a part of the contract closeout
procedure, but whether it is or not, the project can't be formally
closed until the system is accepted.

The Contract Closeout

Contracts require a lot of administrative effort to execute, and
closing one usually means that some specific forms, letters, and/
or reports have to be generated. Often, particularly with federal
sector contracts, the formal acceptance of a system is a part of the
contract closeout procedure. This procedure is done with a letter
or with a standard form that gives the contract name and number,
date of acceptance, and the signature of the designated contracting officer.

The contract closeout also might involve the return of equipment owned by the customer. In very large, expensive, or highly
developmental projects, it is not unusual for the customer to supply specialized equipment such as tools, test equipment, computers, or special software to aid in developing the system. If this is
the case, this equipment either must be returned to the customer
or disposed of in accordance with the contract provisions. Often,
it is cheaper for the customer to allow the contractor to keep the
equipment than to ship it back, but however it is disposed of, you
must formally account for this equipment.

Administratively, disposing of the customer-furnished equipment is part of the contract closeout; physically it is a part of the
office closeout.

The Office Closeout

Many projects are executed on-site, which means that the contractor works on the project at the customer's location. Often the
customer provides an office or workspace for the project, but usu-

ally on-site means that the contractor has to lease office and workspace within a specified radius of the customer's location. If the project is actually accomplished on the customer's premises, there may not be much site-closing activity required beyond the removal of personal belongings and company equipment. Otherwise, the project manager will have to close out the lease, stop all utilities, disconnect telephone service, and notify all suppliers. In either case, the project manager is responsible for packing and shipping the company-owned and customer-owned supplies and equipment back to the parent company or to the designated customer ship point.

Lessons Learned

Most companies do a poor job of capturing the lessons learned from their projects. There is a natural tendency to rush team members, and even the project manager, off to new projects. Once a project is completed, it is difficult to regroup the team for the two or three hours it takes to complete a lessons-learned analysis. The irony is that most of the data already exists in the form of status reports and other project documents. It only requires tapping into the collective memory and project experiences of the team to complete the analysis. If the status and other reports are thorough and capture information that actually describes what happened within the project during the reporting period, then summarizing the information in a final lessons-learned document is relatively easy and painless.

Personnel Reassignment

Although the project manager has no functional authority over project personnel, he should make every reasonable effort to facilitate reassignment to other projects as each individual's work is finished. There are two reasons why getting team members reassigned should be a priority with the project manager: First, it is the right thing to do. Second, it will pay enormous dividends for both the project manager and the organization in the future.

One of the reports that the project manager will submit during closeout is a personnel report. Since the project manager has no functional authority over team personnel, he is not the person to write performance reviews. However, the project manager is often asked to make comments for an individual's performance review. This is because he will have observed the individual's work and team behavior at close hand. In the same vein, the project manager should submit a personnel report to all the appropriate functional managers, detailing each individual's work ethic, team skills, technical expertise, and whether the person should be assigned to future projects. Obviously, this report should have limited and confidential distribution.

Closing and Archiving Files

Good project managers will maintain two types of files—the project book, which is the collection of all the project-related plans, reports, and any other pertinent documentation, and the contract files, which contain all the legal documentation relative to the project. Like the lessons-learned report, the project book and contract files contain vital historical data that should be maintained in a useable and accessible format for future reference. Most organizations now maintain these documents in an electronic format, which greatly facilitates accessibility. Being user-friendly also encourages other teams to refer to and use this historical record as well.

Closing the books on the project requires one final report, which is referred to as the final project audit. This is essentially a compilation of the other reports we mentioned above and, in fact, can be thought of as the cover page that forwards these other reports. A sample format for the final project audit is shown in Exhibit 11-3. Notice that this format can serve the dual purpose of being a checklist for the project manager of closeout activities, as well as being a report format.

Final Project Audit Report

I.   Executive Summary
II.   Introduction
III.   Project Review
IV.   Planning Effectiveness
V.   Project Management Effectiveness
VI.   Effectiveness of Technical Solutions
VII.   Project Deliverables
VIII. Quality
IX.   Schedule
X.   Finances
XI.   Resources Utilization
XII.   Individual Team Member Assessment and Recommendations
        (Submit as separate, confidential report)
XIII. Lessons Learned
XIV. Recommendations

Exhibit 11-3. Sample final project audit format.

Once this final project audit report is compiled, it is sent to all the project stakeholders and is included in the project archives.

Preparing for Product Maintenance

Information technology is one of those industries where the project is finished and delivered but still has a connection to the providing organization. In other words, the customer expects, and pays for, a continuing maintenance of the system after it is delivered.

Organizationally, the best way to set up and plan for continuing product maintenance is to have the specialist groups that do the initial project management activities design and develop the product and specialist groups that will maintain the product once it is shipped. This is a statement of the obvious, so what is the big deal? The big deal is that too often organizations fail to adequately plan for and execute a smooth hand-off between these two groups. The project team that develops the product has to close the project with the approach that its documentation is essentially the statement of requirements and statement of scope for the maintenance team. That is why I believe project life cycles should actually have a final cycle phase that is devoted to continuing product and service maintenance. If we view all our projects from this perspective, then the final phase will require some overlap of activities between the development project team and the maintenance project teams. This results in a better IT system for the customer.

Summary

The closeout phase of the project life cycle is as important as any other phase, yet many project mangers and their organizations do not place as much value on this phase as it deserves. The primary reason is that any project-oriented organization that is especially dependent on external contracts for their core business is under enormous competitive pressure to move on to new projects as quickly as possible. This usually means that functional managers start reassigning project team members to new projects even before their old assignment is completed.

The project manager must plan for the closeout phase well in advance of the schedule project end—ideally in the development phase of the project life cycle. And the project manager must resist, within realistic boundaries, the siphoning off of team members before a formal project close date. Since the project manager does not have functional authority over the team members, this is not easy to do. One thing that can help is to include the closeout requirements and responsibilities in the project charter.

Although the primary emphasis in any project is to provide the end product to the customer on time and on schedule, the project manager must not forget that there are ancillary support items required in each project. For instance, almost every project requires documentation such as operating manuals. The project manager has to ensure that all requirements of the project *and* the product are satisfied.

Finally, one important task in the closeout phase that is often overlooked is the final audit or evaluation. This important task is critical to the organization because it is from these audits that future projects can be made better. The audit is accomplished principally for the lessons learned that could be applied to future projects.

Chapter 12

Customer Service— Finishing the Project

It takes little to convince an individual, or a company, that customer service is important. After all, as customers each of us expects good service. The problem is that achieving consistently good customer service is not easy. Achieving consistently good customer service as an information technology provider is particularly difficult. An IT provider is in direct and constant contact with the customer or end user and has to be "on" all the time, even, in many cases, twenty-four hours a day. Furthermore, quantifying customer service standards in IT is difficult because the product is multifaceted. Every service action becomes a product in the customer's mind and is separately, if not consciously, evaluated. That is, the process is evaluated as much as the product. Also, depending upon the requirement, service actions are performed by different members of a team. This results in various perceptions of customer service.

The design, development, and implementation of a customer service program involve several steps, each with numerous discrete tasks.

Defining Customer Service

In the broadest sense, customer service is whatever adds to customer satisfaction. This definition probably had its roots in the quality revolution of the 1990s, because one goal of total quality management (TQM) was to give the customer more quality than expected as a way, at least partially, to achieve customer satisfaction. This concept, however, came under fire because it often leads to gold plating, which means giving the customer more than he asks and charging for it. Companies also are learning that quality service and customer service are not necessarily the same thing. The trend now is to provide the customer with exactly what was specified to the defined quality standards. Where does that leave customer service? A service provider can meet contract specifications precisely but still deliver poor service to the customer. Hence, the customer may be satisfied with the product but less than pleased with the provider. As Marc Bird of Kinnarps (UK) Ltd., a global office furniture and management solutions consultant company, says, "There is a difference between satisfying customers and delighting them." Delighting the customer is the essence of customer service.

Customer service means that every employee puts the customer first. In short, the company must be customer-focused. To do this requires corporate commitment, planning, training, and a measurement system with which progress can be determined and service imparted. Exhibit 12-1 graphically depicts the key elements of a customer service program.

Before any useable measuring tool can be applied, a precise definition of customer service is required, and it must be applied uniformly across the company. A search of the literature quickly reveals that there are numerous definitions for customer service, but none apply to every industry or even to every situation within an industry. A definition of customer service that is used as a foundation for this chapter is:

> Customer service means providing service features, acts, and information so the customer can

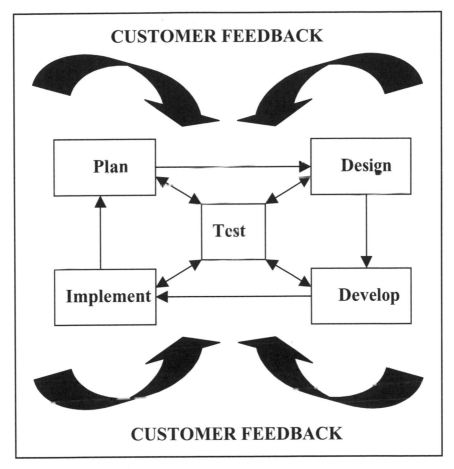

Exhibit 12-1. The customer service development process.

experience the full value of the service or product provided.

I have found that this definition is broad enough to apply to any industry and to any situation we encounter, and it forms the foundation of our program to "delight the customer."

Planning for Customer Service Measurement

Measuring customer service makes no sense until a customer service program is developed and implemented. Many companies have a customer service program that has evolved over a number of years, but usually without any formalized plan or process. However, with increasing competitive pressures, it becomes readily apparent that a formal plan is needed and has to be implemented across the organization.

A recommended way to start the planning process is with a senior officer retreat to foster greater teamwork within the company, as well as to obtain buy-in and commitment to a customer service program. As with any program dealing with changing corporate culture, a customer service program will not work without top-level support and active participation. Once management is on board and there is a clear direction, a customer service plan can be developed and implemented. Although a plan is necessary, it is not completely sufficient.

During the design phase it will become painfully clear that a customer service plan is only as good as the measurement, response, and plan refinement process. Without a way to obtain clear and accurate feedback, a company never knows how good its service is. A prime example of an inadequate measurement program is that of the old, and now defunct, People Express. Just months before the airline was forced into merging with Texas Air because its abominable service had alienated customers, People Express chairman Donald Barr claimed on the television program *Face the Nation* that the airline gave excellent service. Even after the interviewer reminded Mr. Barr that his airline was referred to as People Distress and was considered a joke in the industry, he steadfastly insisted that they provided excellent service. Clearly, People Express had a poorly designed customer feedback process, or it didn't solicit customer feedback at all.

To ensure that the best and most accurate feedback information possible is obtained, most companies have to engineer a new, or reengineer an existing, measurement process. The measurement process is an evolving one and has to be refined and updated on a continuing basis. The five steps toward defining a customer service measurement program are:

1. Identify, understand, and correct plan obstacles.
2. Determine the customer's service expectations.

3. Develop service tactics to meet or exceed the customer's expectations.
4. Develop measurement tools for assessing customer satisfaction.
5. Develop a process for refining the customer service plan.

Identifying, Understanding, and Correcting Plan Obstacles

The first task in developing a customer service measurement program is to identify, understand, and correct the obstacles within the company that can sabotage successful implementation of the program.

Many companies design surveys, score sheets, or other tools and pass them to their customers without ever realizing that the measurement tool itself is a relatively small part of the measurement process. What has to be considered are the people who interface with the customer, the equipment they have to work with, the support they get from the rest of the company, and the training they need to administer and evaluate the measurement instruments. Without this upfront company analysis, the measurement program is doomed to failure. Exhibit 12-2 lists eight typical problems that must be addressed and corrected before a measurement program can be implemented. Most of these problems can be corrected by building a strong team spirit in the company and by getting 100 percent commitment from the senior management. The importance of senior management commitment cannot be emphasized enough. Without it, the program will fail.

Determine the Customer's Service Expectations

Determining the customer's service expectations is key to designing a good customer service measurement program. On the sur-

What Can Go Wrong	What to Do
Inadequate communications between departments, teams, customer, or contractor	Schedule regular team-building sessions and problem-solving meetings.
Employees not rewarded for quality, customer service, or quality effort	Make quality and customer service a performance goal and reward achievement.
Lack of interdepartment support	Usually a result of poor communications. Team-building exercises help but tend to take time. An excellent and more immediate remedy is a project charter issued by the company president describing the project and the expectations of each department.
Understaffing	Understaffing usually is a cost-cutting measure. Tie staffing requirements to customer service and sell to management as a profit enhancement.
Too few or out-of-date information systems	Inadequate or out-of-date equipment is actually more costly in the long term than the cost of new equipment. Provide the best equipment possible.
Inadequate interpersonal skill training	Training for every individual is crucial. Establish budget, identify courses, and schedule employees.
Low morale; no team spirit	Usually a result of poor communication and lack of support. Can be improved with team-building exercises or periodic senior management "town meetings."
Inadequate or poor organizational policies and procedures	Corrected by a regular review and revision of all company policies and procedures.

Exhibit 12-2. Identifying, understanding, and correcting plan obstacles.

face, this might not appear to be a significant item. However, many employees think in terms of quality control, which is a decidedly different concept than quality service. An educational process within the company may be necessary to explain the differences.

The two basic aspects of quality control are whether the product conforms to specifications and its fitness for use. Quality service, on the other hand, does not have such concrete properties against which it can be measured. For instance, it is easy to assess the quality of a car door by determining if it closes properly, but it is not possible to measure the quality service associated with the car until it is bought and used, and a maintenance history is developed. Even then, the quality service is more a function of how the dealer takes care of the car's problem, services it, and treats the buyer than whether the car meets all its specifications. Again, the customer evaluates the process as well as the product.

Develop Service Tactics to Meet or Exceed the Customer's Expectations

Closely tied to the problem of determining the customer's service expectation is developing tactics to meet these expectations. Eight critical tactics for achieving superior service are shown in Exhibit 12-3. Notice that all these tactics, except dealing with delivery systems, are people-oriented and require the development of superior interpersonal skills. It also should be noted that these eight tactics are ongoing and are not sequential; they can be accomplished in any order.

Develop Measurement Tools for Assessing the Customer Service Program

When the first three elements for a good customer service program are in place, the actual design and development of measure-

Tactics	Implementation
Know your customer intimately.	• Make your customer your friend. • Understand the customer's goals and mission. • Be aware of customer budgetary and political pressures.
Find and retain quality people.	• Look for people with superior interpersonal, leadership, and technical skills. • Foster the view that every employee is a marketer and customer service representative. • Provide employees opportunities to exercise their skills and reward their achievements.
Focus your team on the service goals.	• Align service program with company vision and mission goals. • Ensure that employees are clear about job performance and service goals. • Achieve service goals awareness through training, newsletters, service slogan displayed on company stationery, and business cards.
Make business easier with excellent delivery systems.	• Automate work control systems to expedite work orders, record work performance. • Install just-in-time purchasing/inventory systems. • Electronically link corporate and site locations.
Train and support employees.	• Provide comprehensive, multifaceted training for all to stay proficient with customer service procedures, processes, and tools.
Involve and empower employees.	• Push responsibility and authority to lowest level possible to service complaints. • Involve employees in service planning. • Support employee decisions.
Recognize and reward good performance.	• Be sensitive to and reward even small achievements. • Avoid using customer service mistakes to punish employees. • Acknowledge good performance with more than a "well done."
Set the tone and lead the way through personal example.	• *All* senior corporate officers and *all* supervisors have to believe in the customer program and constantly reflect it in the treatment of internal and external customers.

Exhibit 12-3. Elements of superior service tactics.

ment tools can begin. The four most commonly used survey response measurement tools are listed in Exhibit 12-4.

Written Surveys

Two types of written surveys are utilized by effective customer-oriented companies. The first, shown in Exhibit 12-5, is a short scorecard designed to get instantaneous information about a service action response. The second, shown in Exhibit 12-6, is a longer survey designed to provide the customer with information, as well as to obtain in-depth information about the company's customer satisfaction and job performance.

Measurement Tool	Advantages	Disadvantages
Written survey	• Fast • Less expensive than telephone or face-to-face • Easier to administer • Anonymous	• Low response rate; implies less commitment • Can't probe for additional information • People do not like to fill out forms
Telephone survey	• Allows for quick fixes; builds relationships • Allows for clarification and probing • Higher response rate • Allows adjustment of interview level	• More expensive • Exposes interviewer to personal attack • Sometimes customers reluctant to respond negatively
Face-to-face meetings	• Shows company commitment and interest • Allows probing and clarification • Builds relationships • 100% response rate	• Expensive • Increases senior officer absences from day-to-day duties
Internet Web site survey	• Anonymous • Fast • Inexpensive • Easy to administer • Gets feedback not available otherwise	• Very low response rate

Exhibit 12-4. Survey response measurement tools.

SERVICE REQUEST SURVEY

XYZ Technologies, Inc.

Please rate each statement according to the following scale, and place your answer in the blank provided. This information will help us improve our quality of customer service to you.

> 3 = Excellent
> 2 = Good
> 1 = Poor

1. The response to your call was timely.   [ ]
2. The responder was courteous.   [ ]
3. The problem was corrected.   [ ]
4. You were informed of action(s) taken.   [ ]
5. What is your overall assessment of the response?   [ ]

Comments: _____

_____

_____

_____

Your Organization/Company _____

Your Name (Optional) _____ Telephone (Optional) _____

Please follow mailing instructions on the other side of the card. Thank you for taking the time to provide us with your response.

Exhibit 12-5. Sample customer scorecard.

A written survey is the most common measurement tool. Although they are good tools, studies show that on average only 50 percent to 60 percent of written surveys are answered, compared with 70 percent to 80 percent of telephone surveys. The problem with written surveys is that they are hard to design. They should be constructed so that the customer can quickly fill a survey out and still provide useful information.

Some key questions to ask in a survey are shown in Exhibit 12-7. It is important to include one or two open-ended questions to allow the customer to expand or clarify a concern, if she is inclined to do so. The goal in survey tool design is to provide a rigorous instrument that is user-friendly and evokes honest and candid responses.

REPORT AND SURVEY CARD

WORK STATUS   DATE: _____

Here is a status report on the repairs/service you recently requested:

[ ]   Completed

[ ]   Started, but not completed:

    [ ]   We'll return on _____

    [ ]   We'll call your office to schedule the remaining work.

[ ]   Not started because the door was locked. Please call the number below to reschedule this work.

The work was performed by _____

Special Instructions: _____

_____

If you have any questions or comments, please contact our customer service representative at _____

_____

Please detach and return this evaluation to our local customer service center or the project manager.

Evaluation of Results: If the repair/service you requested has been completed, please take a minute to answer the questions below. Then drop this survey in your outgoing mail. Your response will help us to better serve you.

Date Performed: _____   Location: _____

Check the box that best describes your answer:

1. Response was timely.   [ ] Excellent   [ ] Good   [ ] Poor
2. Responder was courteous.   [ ] Excellent   [ ] Good   [ ] Poor
3. Problem was corrected.   [ ] Excellent   [ ] Good   [ ] Poor
4. You were informed of action taken.   [ ] Excellent   [ ] Good   [ ] Poor
5. Overall assessment of response.   [ ] Excellent   [ ] Good   [ ] Poor

Comments/Suggestions: _____

_____

_____

Exhibit 12-6. Sample report and survey card.

Survey Question Design	Question Examples
Start with a question that focuses on the critical issues.	What are the most important features of our service (product)?
Ask the customer to list priorities; stay away from numbers.	What actions do you expect when you report a problem?
Probe for annoyances that have not yet become full-blown problems.	What else could have we have done to improve the service rendered?
Try to avoid questions with obvious answers; instead, key on discriminators.	How important is fast response compared with disruption in the workplace? How important is price compared to service action completion?

Exhibit 12-7. Keys to effective survey question design.

Telephone Surveys

Telephone surveys can be expensive but significantly more effective than written surveys. When a company is dependent upon contracts for its livelihood, as opposed to, say, a retail store, telephone surveys are 100 percent responsive. That is, contract officers and project officers are always willing to talk about the contract, and most of them appreciate corporate involvement. That does not mean that all customer representatives are completely candid. Eliciting usable information still requires excellent interpersonal skills and knowledge about how to ask the right questions. But the opportunities for clarification and probing are significantly greater over the telephone and provide the added bonus of establishing lasting relationships, if conducted effectively.

The Face-to-Face Meeting

The most effective customer service tool is a face-to-face meeting because it provides an opportunity to probe deeper than written surveys, and you can assess the customer's body language. In addition, and perhaps more important, it provides an opportunity to build the trust that leads to long-term relationships.

The most successful customer-oriented organizations have senior management teams routinely visit their customers. The most effective visits are informal and designed to solicit off-the-record customer information about the company's performance. The customer reacts positively to senior management visits because they demonstrate a company's commitment and that senior management listens to customer complaints.

Internet Web Site Surveys

Many companies are designing Web pages and making themselves available electronically. Even though the Web site survey is not used as much as other formats, it is a valuable measurement tool because of the feedback it elicits that wouldn't be available any other way. The anonymity of the Web page makes it more appealing to some people. It also opens the company to comment from a wider audience, namely users as well as direct customers. At this time, unfortunately, response to Web site surveys is low. However, it is bound to become a more popular response format as Web page design improves and we learn more about how to solicit feedback.

Developing a Process for Refining the Customer Service Plan

The goal of a customer service plan is to capture current and accurate feedback from the customer and to utilize this feedback to constantly refine and improve the entire customer service program. There are six key principles to remember about customer feedback:

1. Feedback is tied to service goals.
2. It is both qualitative and quantitative.
3. Feedback is immediate.
4. It goes to the person performing the job or task.
5. It goes to all levels of the organization, when relevant.
6. Feedback is graphically represented for greater impact and understanding.

But there are three crucial questions that must be asked when eliciting feedback: What should we stop doing? What should we start doing? What should we continue doing?

The development and implementation of a superior measurement system requires a lot of effort. It also may take several months of refinement before it provides the information needed by the company. But without superior assessment, superior customer service is not likely.

Summary

Customer service is service that delights the customer. Simply satisfying a customer does not necessarily make a loyal customer.

A major problem in most customer service programs lies in determining how to measure the extent of a customer's satisfaction. There are four common tools used in today's measurement system: written surveys, telephone surveys, face-to-face meetings, and Web site surveys. Working together, they provide significant feedback for refining and improving the customer service program.

The key point to remember about measuring customer satisfaction is that dissatisfied customers often do not express their dissatisfaction—they simply leave. Hence, a superior customer service measurement program is one that is constantly tested and improved to capture current feedback and keep the customer coming back.

Index

269